BRIGHAM
YOUNG

THE CHELSEA HOUSE LIBRARY OF BIOGRAPHY

BRIGHAM YOUNG

BOB BERNOTAS

Chelsea House Publishers

New York • Philadelphia

CHELSEA HOUSE PUBLISHERS

Editor-in-Chief   Remmel Nunn
Managing Editor   Karyn Gullen Browne
Copy Chief   Mark Rifkin
Picture Editor   Adrian Allen
Art Director   Maria Epes
Assistant Art Director   Howard Brotman
Manufacturing Director   Gerald Levine
Systems Manager   Lindsey Ottman
Production Manager   Joseph Romano
Production Coordinator   Marie Claire Cebrián

The Chelsea House Library of Biography
Senior Editor   Kathy Kuhtz

Staff for **BRIGHAM YOUNG**
Associate Editor   Scott Prentzas
Copy Editor   Christopher Duffy
Editorial Assistant   Michele Berezansky
Picture Researcher   Pat Burns
Series Designer   Basia Niemczyc
Cover Illustration   Howard Brotman

Printed and bound in Mexico.

First Printing

1   3   5   7   9   8   6   4   2

Library of Congress Cataloging-in-Publication Data

Bernotas, Bob
Brigham Young/by Bob Bernotas; with an introduction
by Vito Perrone.
   p. cm.—(The Chelsea House library of biography)
Includes bibliographical references and index.
Summary: A biography of the famous Mormon leader and president of the
Church of Jesus Christ of Latter-Day Saints.
ISBN 0-7910-1642-0
      0-7910-1646-3 (pbk.)
1. Young, Brigham, 1801–1877—Juvenile literature. 2. Mormon Church—
Presidents—Biography—Juvenile literature. 3. Church of Jesus Christ of
Latter-Day Saints—Presidents—Biography—Juvenile literature. [1.Young,
Brigham, 1801–1877. 2. Mormon Church—Presidents. 3. Church of Jesus
Christ of Latter-Day Saints—Presidents.] I. Title. II. Series.
BX8695.Y7B47 1992   91-21199
289.3'092—dc20   CIP
   [B]   AC

Contents

Learning from Biographies—*Vito Perrone*   7

1   This Is the Right Place   11

2   A Poor Boy and a Poor Man   25

3   I Feel Like Shouting Hallelujah   37

4   Joseph Was a Prophet, and I Knew It   49

5   Appointed by the Finger of God   65

6   The Kingdom of God or Nothing   81

7   To Die in Harness   95

Further Reading   107

Chronology   108

Index   110

THE CHELSEA HOUSE LIBRARY OF BIOGRAPHY

Barbara Bush

John C. Calhoun

Clarence Darrow

Charles Darwin

Anne Frank

William Lloyd Garrison

Raisa Gorbachev

Martha Graham

J. Edgar Hoover

Saddam Hussein

Jesse James

Rose Kennedy

John Lennon

Jack London

Horace Mann

Edward R. Murrow

William Penn

Edgar Allan Poe

Norman Schwarzkopf

Joseph Smith

Sam Walton

Frank Lloyd Wright

Boris Yeltsin

Brigham Young

Other titles in the series are forthcoming.

Learning from Biographies

Vito Perrone

The oldest narratives that exist are biographical. Much of what we know, for example, about the Pharaohs of ancient Egypt, the builders of Babylon, the philosophers of Greece, the rulers of Rome, the many biblical and religious leaders who provide the base for contemporary spiritual beliefs, has come to us through biographies—the stories of their lives. Although an oral tradition was long the mainstay of historically important biographical accounts, the oral stories making up this tradition became by the 1st century A.D. central elements of a growing written literature.

In the 1st century A.D., biography assumed a more formal quality through the work of such writers as Plutarch, who left us more than 500 biographies of political and intellectual leaders of Rome and Greece. This tradition of focusing on great personages lasted well into the 20th century and is seen as an important means of understanding the history of various times and places. We learn much, for example, from Plutarch's writing about the collapse of the Greek city-states and about the struggles in Rome over the justice and the constitutionality of a world empire. We also gain considerable understanding of the definitions of morality and civic virtue and how various common men and women lived out their daily existence.

Not surprisingly, the earliest American writing, beginning in the 17th century, was heavily biographical. Those Europeans who came to America were dedicated to recording their experience, especially the struggles they faced in building what they determined to be a new culture. John Norton's *Life and Death of John Cotton*, printed in 1630, typifies these early works. Later biographers often tackled more ambitious projects. Cotton Mather's *Magnalia Christi Americana*, published in 1702, accounted for the lives of more than 70 ministers and political leaders. In addition, a biographical literature around the theme of Indian captivity had considerable popularity. Soon after the American Revolution and the organization of the United States of America, Americans were treated to a large outpouring of biographies about such figures as Benjamin Franklin, George Washington, Thomas Jefferson, and Aaron Burr, among others. These particular works served to build a strong sense of national identity.

Among the diverse forms of historical literature, biographies have been over many centuries the most popular. And in recent years interest in biography has grown even greater, as biography has gone beyond prominent government figures, military leaders, giants of business, industry, literature, and the arts. Today we are treated increasingly to biographies of more common people who have inspired others by their particular acts of courage, by their positions on important social and political issues, or by their dedicated lives as teachers, town physicians, mothers, and fathers. Through this broader biographical literature, much of which is featured in THE CHELSEA HOUSE LIBRARY OF BIOGRAPHY, our historical understandings can be enriched greatly.

What makes biography so compelling? Most important, biography is a human story. In this regard, it makes of history something personal, a narrative with which we can make an intimate connection. Biographers typically ask us as readers to accompany them on a journey through the life of another person, to see some part of the world through another's eyes. We can, as a result, come to understand what it is like to live the life of a slave, a farmer, a textile worker, an engineer, a poet, a president—in a sense, to walk in another's shoes. Such experience can be personally invaluable. We cannot ask for a better entry into historical studies.

Although our personal lives are likely not as full as those we are reading about, there will be in most biographical accounts many common experiences. As with the principal character of any biography, we are also faced with numerous decisions, large and small. In the midst of living our lives we are not usually able to comprehend easily the significance of our daily decisions or grasp easily their many possible consequences, but we can gain important insights into them by seeing the decisions made by others play themselves out. We can learn from others.

Because biography is a personal story, it is almost always full of surprises. So often, the personal lives of individuals we come across historically are out of view, their public personas masking who they are. It is through biography that we gain access to their private lives, to the acts that define who they are and what they truly care about. We see their struggles within the possibilities and limitations of life, gaining insight into their beliefs, the ways they survived hardships, what motivated them, and what discouraged them. In the process we can come to understand better our own struggles.

As you read this biography, try to place yourself within the subject's world. See the events as that person sees them. Try to understand why the individual made particular decisions and not others. Ask yourself if you would have chosen differently. What are the values or beliefs that guide the subject's actions? How are those values or beliefs similar to yours? How are they different from yours? Above all, remember: You are engaging in an important historical inquiry as you read a biography, but you are also reading a literature that raises important personal questions for you to consider.

Mormon pioneers pause during their migration to Salt Lake City in 1866. Nineteen years earlier, Brigham Young had led the first group of Mormon settlers to their new home in present-day Utah. There he supervised the building of a vast community where Mormons could live free from persecution.

1

This Is the Right Place

IN THE YEAR 1844, the Church of Jesus Christ of Latter-day Saints, whose members are better known as Saints or Mormons, had arrived at a crossroads in its 14-year history. As the Mormon settlement of Nauvoo, Illinois, grew, so did the anti-Mormon prejudices of its neighbors. Just a few years earlier, their zealously defended, nonconformist beliefs had inflamed anti-Mormon passions in Missouri. Thousands of Saints had been expelled from the state by force in 1838 and 1839. Now, in Nauvoo, the town in western Illinois founded by these Missouri exiles, the same drama was about to be replayed.

On June 27, 1844, an anti-Mormon mob murdered the religion's founder and prophet, Joseph Smith, and his brother, Hyrum, as they awaited trial in a Carthage, Illinois, jail cell. By mid-August, 43-year-old Brigham Young—a devout Mormon, a skillful organizer and administrator, and a devoted follower of the slain prophet—had established himself as the new head of the Mormon church.

As early as 1842, Joseph Smith had realized that the Saints would not be able to remain in Illinois forever. The martyred leader's fears became a painful reality in January 1845, when the Illinois legislature, responding to widespread anti-Mormon sentiment in the state, revoked the Nauvoo city charter. That the Mormons now were facing another exodus, a second forced removal of the church and its followers from an all too brief sanctuary, was plain to Smith's successor, Brigham Young. With their destination still not decided upon, Young began to prepare the Mormons for their westward migration. In September 1845, he announced that the Saints would start to evacuate Nauvoo by the spring of the following year.

Once the Saints left Nauvoo, however, the going was very slow. By mid-June 1846, the lead company, which consisted of 500 wagons and 2,500 of the faithful, had gotten only as far as the Missouri River. This group—which set up camp at present-day Council Bluffs, Iowa—had traveled only three miles a day. Behind them, 3,000 wagons carrying as many as 15,000 Mormons were spread across the prairie of the Iowa Territory.

Young and the other Mormon leaders were faced with a serious decision about the future of the journey. At its slow rate of travel, it could take the huge party years to reach the western frontier beyond the Rocky Mountains. They simply did not have enough provisions to last that long. Young proposed that a pilot company of 200 to 500 young men without families be sent ahead. The rest of the migrants would settle for the winter of 1846–47 and plant crops. The Mormons crossed the Missouri River and established a temporary community located six miles north of the present-day city of Omaha, Nebraska. They named it Winter Quarters.

At this point, there no longer was any doubt, either in Young's mind or his people's, about where he was leading them. He planned to dispatch the pilot company to the Bear River valley in the Great Basin, where the present-day state of Utah is located. This would be the Saints' final gathering place, a sanctuary where there were no potentially hostile settlers who could arouse anti-Mormon persecution and once again force their expulsion.

Young's plan was disrupted in late June 1846, when he received a surprising request. President James K. Polk, then in the midst of directing the nation's efforts in the Mexican-American War, called for a battalion of Mormon volunteers to march west to California. The pragmatic Mormon leader realized that it would be in his people's best interests to do what the president had asked. Mobilizing the battalion, Young reasoned, would demonstrate Mormon support for the United States at a time when many Americans were questioning the group's loyalty to the nation.

There also were material considerations: After a year's service, the men would be mustered out with weapons and, more important, money that could be used to finance this

In February 1846, the Mormons cross the Mississippi River on the ice. Violence directed toward Mormons compelled the controversial religious group to abandon Nauvoo, the community that they had founded in 1839.

In 1846, President James K. Polk asked Young to organize a battalion of Mormon volunteers to fight in the Mexican-American War. Wishing to improve the strained relations between the Mormons and the federal government, the Mormon leader agreed to provide the unit.

costly migration. "If we want the privilege of going where we can worship God according to the dictates of our conscience," he concluded, "we must raise the Battalion." So, on July 21, the 526-member Mormon Battalion, clad in the uniform of the U.S. Army, marched out of Winter Quarters and headed toward California.

According to Mormon lore, on January 14, 1847, Young received a revelation from God that gave divine approval to his work in organizing the Mormon migration and instructed him to begin the exodus in the spring. Immediately, Young devoted himself to the task of outfitting the first party of Saints to head west.

He and the other church leaders realized that it would not be possible to lead the entire Winter Quarters settlement across the prairie in one fell swoop. Instead, Young would set out with a pioneer party of "12 times 12 men," a hardy group that could persevere until a sanctuary was found. No one else, except those who could sustain themselves, would be permitted to follow until a crop could be harvested in the Great Basin in 1848.

The pioneer company's main responsibility would be to chart a road into the Great Salt Lake valley for Mormon wagon trains to follow. With the counsel of the top men in the church, Young selected experienced frontiersmen—carpenters, mechanics, blacksmiths, hunters—who possessed the special skills that would be needed on the arduous trek across the desolate prairie and the formidable Rocky Mountains.

Originally, Young intended that the party be entirely male, but his brother Lorenzo insisted that his wife come along. She was a chronic asthmatic, and Lorenzo was afraid to leave her behind. So that she would have company, Young allowed two other women, his wife Clara and the wife of his close friend Heber Kimball, to join the company. During the long journey, the task of gathering fuel for the evening campfires, as well as all the cooking, washing, and sewing for the entire company, was performed by the three women.

At eight o'clock on the morning of Friday, April 14, 1847, 143 men (1 had taken sick and could not leave), 3 women, and 2 children (a son and stepson of Lorenzo Young) left Winter Quarters and began their historic journey. Three of the men were black slaves, who belonged to Mormons from the South. The pioneers traveled in 73 wagons and took along 93 horses, 66 oxen, 52 mules, 19 cows, and assorted dogs, cats, and chickens. They also carried a large cannon to protect themselves against hostile Native Americans.

The company traveled like an army, well organized and disciplined, with Brigham Young as their general. He set down a strict daily routine for the company. Each day, as the bugle sounded reveille at 5:00 A.M., the pioneers would arise and attend prayers before breakfast. The company would

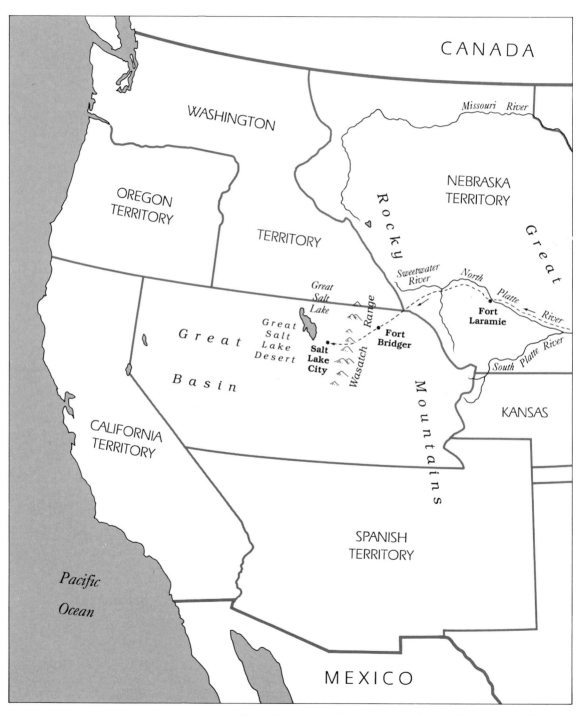

The Mormon Migration from Nauvoo, Illinois,

to Salt Lake City, 1846-7

begin its day's travel by about 7:30 A.M., stopping for an hour around noon. Near the end of each day, Young would ride ahead to select that night's campsite. The Mormons would circle their wagons and camp around 6:30 P.M. After supper, prayers were held at 8:30 P.M., and taps was sounded at 9:00 P.M.

This rigid regimen enabled the Mormon pioneers to cover an average of 10 miles per day—more than 3 times the rate of the previous year's journey from Nauvoo to Winter Quarters. Initially, however, plodding across a trackless prairie that had not yet fully awakened from winter proved a difficult chore. For much of the first week or so, the pioneers had to pull their wagons through soft and sandy loam. The going was slow and monotonous.

Just a few days after leaving Winter Quarters, the Mormons encountered a group of Pawnee Indians. A nomadic people indigenous to Nebraska, the Pawnee were being pushed off their lands by larger tribes, such as the Sioux, as white settlement expanded westward. The Pawnee demanded a gift from the Mormons as a toll for allowing the caravan to cross their land. Young gave them some tobacco, salt, and other provisions, but the Pawnee were not satisfied and stole two horses.

To further harass the Mormons, some Pawnees set fire to the dry grass ahead of the company. If fed by a high wind, a prairie fire might become a wall of flame 20 feet high and could overtake a slow-moving wagon train. Young and his people were extremely fortunate that the fire caused them no harm.

In early May, the Mormon pioneers caught their first sight of buffalo. At once, the wagons halted, and a band of hunters sped toward the herd. They enjoyed the meat greatly, finding it, in the words of one of the party, "very sweet and [as] tender as veal." The Saints liked the taste of buffalo perhaps too much; as they traveled, the hunters killed an increasing number of the huge beasts until the camp had an overabundance of meat. Young was disturbed when he learned that good meat was being thrown away. He ordered all his people to stop this indiscriminate hunting, expressing a rare concern—for a white man—for the ecology of the prairie. "God has given us a Commandment," he told them sternly, "that we should not waste meat, nor take life unless it is needed."

In late May, the Mormons were met by a band of about 35 Sioux. Unlike the Pawnee, they gladly accepted the Saints' gifts, and the encounter was in no way hostile or tense. The company was making fine progress by this time, but Young had become concerned over what he observed as a growing laxity within the camp. Having left their families behind at Winter Quarters, the male pioneers grew irresponsible and careless. They spent their leisure time joking profanely and laughing loudly, as they played cards, checkers, or dominoes in their wagons. Many had brought musical instruments, which they played raucously while their listeners danced, hoedown style, to the lighthearted music.

Young found this behavior offensive; they were, after all, on their way to create the Kingdom of God on earth. On the morning of May 29, 1847, he summoned the camp together and spoke his mind. "Joking, nonsense, profane language,

A Native American hunting party surrounds a buffalo herd on the Great Plains. On their journey west, Young and the Mormons crossed the Great Plains; they encountered friendly and hostile groups of Native Americans and hunted buffalo to supplement their food provisions.

trifling conversation, and loud laughter," he rebuked them, "do not belong to us. . . . I am ashamed of it." He warned them that their careless ways would lead only to harm. "If we don't repent and quit our wickedness," Young predicted, "we will have more hindrances than we have had, and worse storms to encounter."

He called a prayer meeting and a fast for the next day, Sunday, in order that the wayward pioneers might "humble ourselves and turn to the Lord and He will forgive us." On that day, after the fasting and prayer—and a brief rain shower—the penitent travelers saw a rainbow. To them, it was a gleaming, multicolored gateway, a sign of forgiveness and welcome to their new home.

On June 2, 1847, the Mormons arrived at Fort Laramie, a major way station for pioneers traveling along the Platte River. The superintendent of the American Fur Company, a French trapper named James Bordeaux, warned Young that if he continued on the north side of the Platte, the passage eventually would be blocked by the Black Hills. Heeding Bordeaux's advice, which was geographically inaccurate, Young decided to cross the river and immediately take his people down the Oregon Trail. Two days later, the Saints rented Bordeaux's flatboat for $15 to ferry the wagons across the Platte and started on the final leg of their journey, the 350-mile trip across present-day Wyoming from Fort Laramie to Fort Bridger.

This was to prove the most challenging phase of the exodus. Because the Oregon Trail was crowded with pioneers heading to California and Oregon, the Mormons found it more difficult than before to secure choice campsites and adequate grazing for their livestock. The trail was rugged, and the Saints had to cross and recross the Platte three different times. Encountering a barren stretch between the Platte and Sweetwater rivers, they endured poor campsites, bad water, and little green grass. Days were hot and nights were cold. As the party climbed to an elevation of 7,750 feet, the air grew thin.

Jim Bridger was the first white man to visit the Great Salt Lake. When the legendary frontiersman met Young and the Mormons on their westward trek in 1847, he told them that he thought the climate of the Salt Lake valley was too cold to grow crops.

Along the way, the Mormons met two of the West's most famous mountain men. The first, Moses "Black" Harris, told them that the Salt Lake region was a sandy, barren, and treeless wasteland, a most unfavorable spot for a settlement. The next day, however, Jim Bridger, the first white man to visit the Great Salt Lake, challenged much of Harris's gloomy picture. The land, Bridger insisted, was mineral rich and well vegetated with plenty of grass, timber, and wild fruit. Still, he warned that the local Indians, the Ute, were hostile toward white settlers and that the climate was too cold to grow crops. "I'll give you $1,000," he wagered

Young, "for the first bushel of corn you grow in the Great Salt Basin." Young quietly replied, "Wait and we will show you."

The Mormons were not deterred by these sobering reports, however, and they pushed on, arriving at Fort Bridger on July 7. There they traded for provisions and repaired their wagons in preparation for the final phase of their long trek. Departing Fort Bridger, they left the Oregon Trail and turned southwest through the Hastings Cutoff for their final descent into the valley of the Great Salt Lake.

Here they met yet another mountain man, Miles Goodyear, who lived near present-day Ogden, Utah—50 miles north of the Saints' ultimate destination. Contradicting both Harris and Bridger, Goodyear insisted that the region offered great agricultural potential and described the abundance of his own vegetable garden. The Mormons proceeded with renewed confidence.

As they neared the end of their journey, the company was struck by an outbreak of what they called "mountain fever." The nausea, headaches, high temperatures, and delirium may have been caused either by the high altitude, mineral salts from the lakes they passed, ticks, or perhaps a combination of all three. No one died, but many were violently ill and remained weak and listless even after they recovered.

Mormon pioneers get their first glimpse of their new home in the West. Within 3 months of the Mormons' arrival in the Great Basin, Salt Lake City was already a well-organized community of nearly 2,000 people.

When Young fell ill, the Mormon travelers were filled with dread. His temperature grew so high that those who were taking care of him began to fear for his life.

On July 13, an advance party of 23 wagons and 42 of the most able men rode out ahead of the main group, through the mountains and toward the Great Basin. Four days later, Young had become so ill that the camp decided they must leave their leader behind with enough people to care for him. The rest of the company would set out, join up with the advance party, and find fertile ground where they could begin planting potatoes, turnips, buckwheat, and other crops. By the morning of July 23, the pioneers had set up camp and began turning the soil, building a dam, and cutting trenches to carry water for irrigation.

The next day, Young, improving but still weak, asked the driver of his carriage to turn the vehicle so he could get a better view. At that moment, the Mormon leader first glimpsed the Great Salt Lake valley, 40 miles long, 20 miles wide, and surrounded by purple, snowcapped mountains. It was nothing like Nauvoo, the green, wooded area along the Mississippi River that they had left more than two years and thousands of miles earlier. Dry and desolate, its barrenness certainly would discourage anyone but the Mormons from settling there. Peering out across the yellowed grass, Young was content in the knowledge that his people already were hard at work building the frontier sanctuary to which he had brought them. "It is enough," he declared with satisfaction. "This is the right place. Drive on."

On July 25, 1847, the first Sunday that the Mormons spent in the Great Basin, the pioneers gathered to pray and give thanks. At the end of the day, Young, basking in the successful completion of his task, addressed the gathered faithful. He exhorted them to follow God's will and warned them to avoid evil; for those who did not heed his words, "nothing but burning through hell would cleanse them." From his strong words and confident manner the Saints could see that although still weak of voice, their leader was himself again.

Brigham Young posed for this portrait in 1850. Looking back on the adversities that he experienced during his youth, Young recalled, "Instead of going to school, I had to chop logs, to sow and plant, to plow in the midst of roots barefooted, and if I had a pair of pants that would cover me I did pretty well."

2

A Poor Boy and a Poor Man

BRIGHAM YOUNG WAS BORN ON June 1, 1801, in the newly founded frontier community of Whitingham, Vermont. He was the ninth of 11 children born to John and Abigail Young. Just five months earlier, his parents had moved their large family from Massachusetts in the hope that they might be able to scratch out an existence by farming the rocky, hilly earth of southern Vermont.

Both of his parents came from sturdy New England stock. During the first half of the 18th century, John Young's ancestors had achieved prominence and respectability in the colony of Massachusetts and were active in business, civil, and religious affairs. His mother's family, the Howes, also were involved in political and religious activities in and around Hopkinton, Massachusetts, and her father was a respected farmer there. Her most famous relative, Elias Howe, Jr., invented the sewing machine.

John Young's father, a surgeon and farmer, was a gambler and a heavy drinker. He died in 1769, leaving a widow, 10 children, and a pile of

Paying tribute to Young's extraordinary character and abilities ("equipment"), this historical marker indicates the site in Whitingham, Vermont, where the Mormon leader was born in 1801.

unpaid bills. Young's farm and all of his possessions were confiscated and sold to pay his debts, and the family was split up. Six-year-old John and his four-year-old brother were indentured as servants to a wealthy Hopkinton landowner, who treated them cruelly and harshly.

In 1780, John Young, then 17 years old, left his master and enlisted in the Continental army. During the final year of the American Revolution, he served in three campaigns under the command of General George Washington. When the war ended in 1781, he returned to Hopkinton, where he met Abigail Howe, known to everyone as Nabby. Her parents objected to their courtship, believing that this former servant, the son of a debtor, was beneath their daughter.

Nevertheless, John Young and Nabby Howe were married in 1785. They lived in the neighboring town of Ashland, where Young worked as a craftsman and mill worker.

Times were hard for John Young and his growing family. By the late 1780s they had moved to Durham, on the eastern side of the Catskill Mountains in New York State, where Young decided to try his hand at farming. Economic difficulties, however, forced the family to return to Hopkinton in 1790. The Youngs remained there for a little more than 10 years, until they moved to Whitingham, Vermont, in January 1801, a few months before the birth of their son, Brigham.

As a farmer, John Young was no more successful in Vermont than he had been in New York. Much of the time, he and his older sons had to hire themselves out to more prosperous farmers so that the family could survive. His older daughters wove straw hats, which they sold for grocery money. In 1804, the Youngs abandoned the rocky New England soil and their hard, humiliating existence and decided to try their luck with the rich earth of upstate New York. Joining the mass migration of New Englanders, the family settled in the rapidly growing town of Smyrna. Once again, however, John Young proved that he was a lackluster farmer, and the family income was chronically meager and precarious.

Brigham spent his childhood and adolescence in the midst of this frontier poverty. "I have been a poor boy and a poor man," he recalled years later, "and my parents were poor. I was poor during my childhood and grew to manhood poor and destitute." By his own account, he received little formal schooling; he learned reading and writing from his mother. Even as a boy, most of his days were consumed by backbreaking labor—logging and driving a team of horses—through both winter and summer. Sometimes he worked on his father's farm, but more often he, like his brothers, was hired out to others. Throughout his difficult youth, Brigham was thankful for small things. "If I had a pair of pants that would cover me," he looked back with an amused sadness, "I did pretty well."

In 1813, the Youngs moved 50 miles west, to Genoa, New York, near the shores of Cayuga Lake. Because John Young was unable to purchase land for farming, he was forced to take work as a hired hand or to labor at other menial tasks. Brigham, then 12 years old, contributed to family meals by hunting and fishing, and, as in Smyrna, he once again was hired out.

John and Nabby Young were people of deep religious convictions, which they passed on to all their children. Brigham's father—an austere, strict Methodist—told his children that activities such as dancing, and even listening

to fiddle music, would put them on the highway to hell. He stringently observed the Sabbath; Sunday walks could not last longer than a half an hour and were to be taken for exercise only, not for pleasure. John Young also supported the growing temperance movement, motivated not only by his devout beliefs but also by the painful memories of early life in servitude, the consequence of his father's drinking.

Every bit as religious as her husband, Nabby Young was not as severe in the practice of her beliefs. She strove to infuse her children with a firm sense of Christian morality, straight from the Bible. "She advised," Young remembered with admiration, "'Read it, observe its precepts and apply them to your lives as far as you can. Do everything that is

A New England farm around the time of Young's birth in 1801. Growing up amid frontier poverty, Young worked on his family's farm and began laboring as a farmhand for wealthy landholders before he reached his teens.

good; do nothing that is evil; and if you see any person in distress, administer to their wants; never suffer anger to rise in your bosom, for if you do, you may be overcome by evil!'"

Just after Brigham's birth, Nabby Young suffered her first spell of consumption, a chronically debilitating lung disease known today as tuberculosis. Never fully healthy afterward, she continued to endure periodic bouts with the sickness, growing gradually weaker through the next 14 years. (A daughter, also named Nabby, succumbed to the disease in 1807.) Finally, on June 11, 1815, she died—10 days after Brigham's 14th birthday.

The entire Young family, and no one more than Brigham, would miss the softening influence that Nabby Young had on her dour, stern husband. After her death, the family moved once again, this time to a site about 35 miles southwest of Genoa, where Brigham's father purchased 100 acres of land thick with maple trees. John Young, however, was no more successful as a producer of maple sugar than he had been as a farmer, and poverty remained the family's constant companion.

Hard work, strict discipline, and the loss of his beloved mother took their toll on Brigham. He fell into a period of deep depression, feeling, as he recalled, "cast down, gloomy, and desponding with everything wearing to me. . . . I felt lonesome and bad."

In 1816, John Young married a widow with several children of her own, abandoned his farm, and by the next year had told the 16-year-old Brigham, "You now have your time; go and provide for yourself." Brigham set out for Auburn, New York, where he initially worked on local farms as a hired hand. But the repeated failures of his father left Brigham with little taste for farming, so he quickly gave up on the countryside and headed for town. There he apprenticed in a woodworking shop and learned the trades of carpentry, painting, and glazing.

The general economic decline of the late 1810s caused great disruption in frontier towns such as Auburn, and

Young soon found himself uprooted again. In 1823, he moved to Port Byron, New York, a growing community on the soon-to-be-completed Erie Canal. Over the next five years, he worked around the town at a number of different jobs, such as repairing chairs, laboring in factories, and building boats. Years of arduous outdoor work had built him into a strong young man, 5 feet 10 inches tall (a full 7 inches taller than his father), large of frame, and broad of chest.

Around this time, Young met 17-year-old Miriam Works, whose father, like his, was a Massachusetts native and a

Miriam Works was 17 years old when she married Brigham Young on October 5, 1824. The couple lived in several towns in western New York until they settled in Mendon, New York, in 1829.

revolutionary war veteran. They were married on October 5, 1824, and settled in Port Byron, where their first child, Elizabeth, was born in 1825. By 1828, they had moved again, to Oswego, New York, on the shore of Lake Ontario, where Young worked on the construction of a large tannery.

Barely a year later, the ever-mobile Young moved his family west to Mendon, New York, where he started his own furniture-manufacturing business. On land that his father gave him, Young constructed a two-story building. His shop was located on the first floor and contained a collection of water-powered machinery—saws, grindstones, lathes—and a forge for blacksmith work. The modestly furnished family residence occupied the second floor.

Unfortunately, Miriam Young had fallen ill with consumption, and after the couple's first child was born, her health remained poor. The birth of Vilate, the Youngs' second daughter, in 1830 further incapacitated Miriam. As a consequence, Brigham was obliged to spend most of the day taking care of his bedridden wife and two young daughters, as well as doing the household chores that Miriam was too weak to perform. Naturally, with precious little time to devote to furniture making, his business suffered. Young was forced to take part-time work as a day laborer for local farmers, as well as occasional carpentry work when he could get it. As with his father, it appeared that failure and poverty would be Brigham Young's constant companions. The overburdened young man would, however, find salvation—both spiritually and financially—in religion.

Beginning around 1800, at about the same time as Brigham Young's birth, a major religious revival known as the Second Great Awakening had swept through what was then the western portion of the United States, from Kentucky to Vermont. At religious assemblies held throughout the frontier, participants experienced visions, spoke in tongues, danced wildly, fell to the ground in spasmodic rapture, and engaged in wild, frenzied exhibitions of charismatic ecstasy. These evangelical gatherings were known as camp meetings because they were usually held outdoors and attended by people who often camped nearby. This was the religious environment in which Brigham Young was raised.

Throughout his early life, Young's family flirted with many of the Protestant denominations and sects that had sprung up and were competing for converts. Attending camp meetings with his parents, Young, by his own account, "was well acquainted with the Episcopalians, Presbyterians, New Lights, Baptists, Freewill Baptists, Wesleyan and Reform Methodists [and] lived from my youth where I was acquainted with the Quakers as well as the other denominations, and was more or less acquainted with almost every other religious ism."

However, Young was embarrassed and repelled by the usual revival-meeting hysteria—the crying out, the falling on the ground, the speaking in tongues. He held back, refusing to accept any set of religious beliefs merely on the basis of familial or social pressure. Instead, as he later claimed, he made up a prayer of his own: "Lord, preserve me until I am old enough to have solid judgment, and a discreet mind ripened on a good, solid foundation of common sense."

It was not until 1824 that the adult Brigham Young decided to commit himself to a religious faith and joined the Methodist church. The 1820s were years of economic depression in the young United States; during such times, impoverished people, such as Young, often turned toward religion as a way to ease feelings of helplessness and inadequacy brought on by economic failures. In addition, Young later admitted that he had grown tired of being called an "infidel" by his churchgoing friends. He recalled, "I got religion in order to prevent my being any more pestered about it."

His religious commitment eventually grew, and by the end of the decade, Brigham Young had turned to a kind of reformed Methodism. Three of his older brothers, Joseph, John, and Phinehas, were itinerant preachers for the

Outdoor religious gatherings known as camp meetings, such as this one held in 1819, were common in the United States in the early 19th century. Young often attended camp meetings with his parents and became familiar with the teachings of many denominations.

Methodist Episcopal Reform Church. This version of Methodism, quite common on the American frontier, studied the Bible closely in order to learn about and revive the original forms and practices of the Christian church as it had existed during the time of Jesus Christ. Young dedicated himself to this sect and often led the local meetings.

Although his devotion to reformed Methodism was solid and sincere, the religious quest of Brigham Young had not ended; indeed, it had barely begun. The year 1830 would be, for him, a time of eye-opening revelations, a year in which his life would be changed irreversibly. As a consequence, the lives of thousands of other people would also change.

Joseph Smith claimed that on September 21, 1823, the angel Moroni revealed to him the location of gold plates that contained ancient writings narrating the history of a race of people who migrated from Jerusalem to North America six centuries before the birth of Christ.

3

I Feel Like Shouting
Hallelujah

TOWARD THE SUMMER OF 1830, Young began to hear rumors that a man named Joseph Smith in nearby Palmyra, New York, had received a revelation from God in the form of "a new Bible, written upon golden plates." This new scripture was called the Book of Mormon. In June, Smith's brother Samuel arrived in Mendon to preach this new gospel and distribute copies of the Book of Mormon. Phinehas Young read the book, praised it for what he felt was its truthfulness, and passed it around to other family members. His father and sister Fanny were impressed. The budding religion interested his younger brother Brigham as well. However, before committing himself, Brigham Young later admitted, he first wanted to "see whether good common sense was manifest" in the teachings of Joseph Smith.

In many ways, Joseph Smith's early life bore an uncanny resemblance to that of the man who would become his most devoted follower and trusted aide. Smith was born in Sharon, Vermont, on December 23, 1805, not far from the place where Brigham Young had been born four and a half years earlier. As a boy, Smith's family led the same kind of hard life, moving from place to place, constantly plagued by crop failures, disease, business disasters, and frontier poverty. They moved to western New York in 1815, where, like Brigham, 10-year-old Joseph was hired out as a farmhand.

Smith and Young also traveled parallel paths in their spiritual quests. They shared a skepticism toward established, organized religions and were confused by all the competing sects. Moreover, both men possessed the same hope that a return to the rituals and practices of the original Christians would restore the "true" church.

One day, while praying in a grove behind his family's house, 14-year-old Joseph had his first religious experience. He was enveloped by a thick darkness, but then, suddenly, a gleaming pillar of light descended upon him. Out of the brightness appeared a vision of Jesus Christ. The vision instructed Joseph not to join any of the existing sects and prophesied that he was destined for greatness.

According to Mormon lore, three years later, on the night of September 21, 1823, Smith was visited by a messenger from God, the angel Moroni (pronounced more-OWN-eye). The angel told him about gold plates that were buried on a hill nearby. The plates were accompanied by two stones that would enable Smith to translate their ancient writings. The next day he rushed to the supposed site of the plates, but Moroni again appeared and told Smith that he was not ready yet to translate them. The angel paid him three more annual visits, until finally, in 1827, Smith was advised that he now was ready to receive the plates.

For most of the next year, he worked diligently on the translation. The plates, according to Smith, told the story of the journey of a group of people from Jerusalem to North America. The exodus, led by a man named Lehi, occurred some 600 years before the birth of Christ. After arriving in the New World, one of Lehi's sons, Nephi, continued to support his father loyally, while two of Lehi's other sons, Laman and Lemuel, questioned his authority. After Lehi's death, Laman and Lemuel and their followers, known as the Lamanites, broke with Nephi and killed him. For their treachery, God cursed them by turning their skin red. According to Mormon doctrine, the Lamanites were the ancestors of Native Americans.

For 10 centuries, conflict raged between the Nephites and Lamanites, until around A.D. 400, when the Nephites were wiped out in a decisive battle fought near Palmyra, New York, Smith's eventual hometown. The plates that Smith claimed to have dug up and translated were written by a number of important Nephite prophets, one of the most important of whom was named Mormon. Mormon's son, Moroni, was the last of the Nephites. He buried the plates in A.D. 421 and revealed their hiding place to Joseph Smith more than 1,400 years later.

The Book of Mormon, then, is held by Mormons to be Smith's translation of this long-hidden history of the ancient people of America. In the same way that Christians accept the Bible to be the testament of Jesus Christ, Mormons believe that this book is Christ's second testament. As such, it is revered as a clarification of and an expansion on the principles set forth in the Bible.

On April 6, 1830, Smith and six other men established the Church of Jesus Christ of Latter-day Saints, also known

These characters are claimed to represent Smith's transcriptions from the gold plates. When Smith finished his translation of the plates in 1830, he published it as the Book of Mormon, which became the textual foundation for the Church of Jesus Christ of Latter-day Saints.

as the Mormon church. (The term *latter-day* refers to the Mormons' belief that humans are living in their last days on earth and that the second coming of Christ is imminent.) On that day, Smith announced that he was to be called "a seer, a translator, a prophet, an apostle of Jesus Christ, an elder of the church through the will of God the Father, and the grace of your Lord Jesus Christ." In its first month, the church grew to 40 members, as Smith's gospel began to spread throughout the small towns of western New York. Not long afterward, the Young family had their first encounters with Mormonism.

In a number of ways, Brigham Young typified the potential Mormon convert. Young, like many people of his time and place, was confused by the various, competing religious sects that had sprung up since 1800. Mormonism attempted to alleviate this confusion, seeking to revive the rituals of the Christian church as practiced in the time of Christ. As such, it could claim to be the only "true" religion, and its converts accepted this claim.

Moreover, Mormonism offered relief from the severe Puritan tradition in which Young had been raised. The Puritans were followers of the French theologian John Calvin, who taught that humanity was stained irrevocably by original sin. Only a select few, the Puritans believed, would attain a heavenly reward. Everyone else, no matter how righteously they had lived, were condemned to eternal damnation.

Mormonism, however, maintained that one's fate was not predetermined and that people would be judged in heaven according to the way they had lived on earth. This "radical" notion—that people could decide their own spiritual destiny—proved comforting to people of Young's social class, powerless people whose harsh earthly life was limited by economic circumstances beyond their control.

Likewise, the Mormon doctrine of a "lay priesthood," according to which every loyal white adult male was a priest in the church, seemed tailor-made for someone like Young. The son of a failed farmer, himself an unsuccessful businessman, he was a common frontier type—a man who, by no fault of his own, had been robbed of economic and social position. Lacking in social status and recognition, these men found in the Mormon priesthood an even higher kind of status and recognition—a spiritual kind.

At the same time, the new religion emphasized respect for authority. All members were expected to support, with unquestioning loyalty, the church and its leaders, particularly Joseph Smith. This might seem to contradict the rather democratic concept of a lay priesthood, a doctrine that spoke to the frontier people's need for status. However, Mormonism's authoritarian element also fed an important need, the desire for order and stability in the midst of a disorderly and unstable society—a world in which a person might be a farmer one day and a pauper the next.

Mormonism, therefore, had a particular appeal among the impoverished, powerless people of the frontier: people who, like Brigham Young, had been beaten down by economic deprivation, day in, day out, year in, year out. These frontier poor, so in need of comfort and order, so lacking in status and power, were drawn in ever larger numbers to the teachings of Joseph Smith. By offering an appealing mix of tradition and superstition, of authority and empowerment, Mormonism quickly reached a ready and ripe pool of converts throughout frontier America.

One of these likely converts was Brigham Young, who by the end of 1831 was being drawn ever closer to the Mormon faith. In January, Brigham, his wife Miriam, his brother Phinehas, Phinehas's wife Clarissa, and their friend Heber Chase Kimball traveled 130 miles in the cold of winter to Columbia, Pennsylvania, to observe a Mormon congregation. Although many of the people spoke in tongues, to Young's relief they did not engage in the wild, ecstasy-driven behavior that had so disgusted him at the

As her family looks on, a Mormon convert is baptized. Brigham Young was baptized into the Mormon church on April 14, 1832. He later wrote that he accepted Mormonism "for the simple reason that it embraces all truth in heaven and on earth, in the earth, under the earth, and in hell, if there be any truth there."

camp meetings of his youth. After six days among the Mormons, Young was convinced that the new religion was, as he put it, "the Gospel in its purity."

In early April, Young's father and his brothers Phinehas and Joseph were baptized into the Mormon faith and simultaneously ordained into the Mormon priesthood. Then, on April 14, 1832, Brigham Young's conversion to Mormonism became official when he was baptized in the stream behind his home in Mendon. Soon Miriam; Young's brothers Lorenzo and John, Jr.; his sisters Fanny, Rhoda, and Nancy; his brother-in-law John P. Greene; and Heber Kimball and his wife, Vilate, also joined the Mormon church.

Immediately after his conversion, Young told a man for whom he was making some furniture, "I can't finish my work for you here, for from now on I have much more important work to do—preaching the gospel." True to his word, he energetically devoted himself to expanding the Mormon following around Mendon, preaching, baptizing, and building churches throughout the region.

Again, however, personal tragedy entered Young's life. On September 8, 1832, his 27-year-old wife, Miriam, died of consumption, the same illness that had taken his mother. Young and his two daughters moved in with Heber and Vilate Kimball.

Soon after Miriam's death, Brigham, his brother Joseph, and Heber Kimball decided to visit Kirtland, Ohio, a trading and milling center near Cleveland. Joseph Smith had moved there in January 1831, and, according to the principles of Mormonism, had begun to assemble the faithful into a growing Mormon settlement. Upon their arrival, they found Smith in the woods, chopping and hauling lumber.

As he shook Smith's hand for the first time, Young was awestruck by his imposing figure—6 feet 2 inches tall, 212 pounds—his strong and youthful appearance, his deep-set blue eyes, and his charismatic personality. This, he immediately knew, was the right man to build the Kingdom of God on earth. Young always cited his first meeting with the "Prophet of God," as he called Smith, as one of the high points of his life. "I feel like shouting hallelujah, all the time," he later declared, "when I think that I ever knew Joseph Smith."

Smith also found reason to be impressed with Young. That first evening, Young and a group of other Mormons were invited to the prophet's home. After a while, Smith called on Young to pray. Young began to speak in an incomprehensible, previously unheard tongue that the leader announced was "the pure Adamic language," that is, the language spoken by the first man, Adam. Young was gratified by Smith's interpretation of this occurrence.

In December 1832, shortly after his return to Mendon,
Young and his brother Joseph ventured out on a mission to
Canada. There they baptized about 45 converts and organized several congregations. They arrived back in Mendon in February, but in April, Young embarked on a second,

even more successful mission, this time throughout Upstate New York as well as Canada. In July, he traveled to Kirtland, escorting a group of Canadian converts who wanted to settle in the Mormon community. Once again he cherished the opportunity to visit with Joseph Smith.

The Mormon temple at Kirtland, Ohio, bears witness to the earlier presence of a prosperous Mormon community. In September 1833, Young moved his family to Kirtland, where Joseph Smith had begun to assemble the Mormon faithful.

Young married Mary Ann Angell in February 1834, two years after the death of his first wife, Miriam.

For almost two years, Smith had been directing his followers to gather either at Kirtland or at a second Mormon settlement near Independence, Missouri. (According to Smith, Missouri was the location of the Garden of Eden, and, after the second coming of Christ, would be the site of the "New Jerusalem.") Heeding these instructions and wanting to be near his revered leader, Young decided in September 1833 to move his family to Kirtland. Young, his two daughters, along with Heber Kimball and his family, arrived there in early November.

Greeting Young, Smith told him "to go to work and aid in building up Kirtland and never again assist in building up

Gentile [non-Mormon] cities." Young found work within the Mormon community as a carpenter. In February 1834, he married Mary Ann Angell, a 30-year-old convert from Seneca, New York, who he believed would be able to take care of his children, keep his house, and bear the burdens of being the wife of a busy, devoted Mormon minister. Most important, living in Kirtland meant, for Young, "the privilege of listening to the teachings of the Prophet." His course now was clear—he had tied his own life, inextricably and indissolubly, to Smith's.

An 1845 portrait depicts Brigham Young, president of the Twelve Apostles, and his family. With Brigham and his wife Mary Ann are their children (left to right) Joseph, Luna, Brigham, Jr., Mary Ann, Alice, and John Willard.

Joseph Smith, revered as a prophet by the Mormons and reviled as a charlatan by his critics, was a man of considerable energy and charisma. Brigham Young later exclaimed, "I feel like shouting hallelujah all the time, when I think that I ever knew Joseph Smith."

4

Joseph Was a Prophet,
and I Knew It

FROM ITS VERY FIRST DAYS as a new religion in Palmyra, New York, Mormonism met with opposition from the surrounding non-Mormon population, whom the Saints referred to as Gentiles. The local citizens organized a boycott against the first printing of the Book of Mormon. Joseph Smith was hounded into court, pursued by mobs, and taunted as a false prophet. It was a story that would be replayed over and over again throughout the history of the Mormon religion, often with tragic results.

Not long after Brigham Young moved to Kirtland, Ohio, anti-Mormon passions erupted into violence between the Mormons of Jackson County, Missouri, and their Gentile neighbors. The local population was alarmed by the mass influx of Mormon settlers into the region. Smith had taught the Mormons that the town of Independence was their spiritual home-land, their Zion. To rid their communities of the perceived menace presented by the Mormons, vigilante mobs burned Mormon houses, destroyed a Mormon newspaper, and tarred and feathered several prominent Saints. From late 1833 to early 1834, some 1,200 Mormons were expelled from their Missouri homes at gunpoint.

In May 1834, Smith, wishing to reclaim Jackson County for the Mormons, organized about 200 of the Kirtland men into an armed force he named Zion's Camp. The presence of this legion, he hoped, might pressure the local authorities into negotiating a settlement between the Saints and the Gentiles. Young was appointed the commander of a company of 12 men, his first position of responsibility in the Mormon church.

Smith's plan was a disaster. Missouri officials were unreceptive to the Mormon's cause. A heavily armed Gentile vigilante force of 300 positioned itself to attack Zion's Camp. Fortunately for the Saints, a heavy rain and hailstorm delayed the attack and forced the Gentiles to regroup. Then a cholera epidemic ravaged the Mormon camp, leaving 70 ill and 13 dead. By late June, the camp recovered, disbanded, and returned to Kirtland.

For Young, however, the ill-fated Zion's Camp expedition was an opportunity to gain leadership experience and demonstrate his allegiance to Mormonism and Joseph Smith. Smith repaid Young's loyalty when, in February of 1835, he appointed Young to the newly created Quorum (or Council) of Twelve Apostles, known informally as the Twelve. Modeled on the 12 apostles of Jesus Christ, their mission was to promote the expansion of the Mormon church both in the United States and abroad. Heber Kimball, who also was named to the Quorum, recalled that Smith told them that they "should have the power to heal the sick, cast out devils, raise the dead, give sight to the blind . . . and many more things too numerous to mention."

For the next year and a half, Young was absorbed in building, physically as well as spiritually, the Mormon church. Young the missionary made two eastern trips during which, as before, he won many converts and organized new branches throughout upstate New York, New England, and

Canada. In between these missions, Young the carpenter helped construct the Kirtland temple, for which he also designed the interior woodwork. The temple was completed in March 1836 and was dedicated at a joyful, intensely spiritual ceremony.

Young never possessed anything less than absolute faith in the leadership of Joseph Smith; he soon would have ample opportunity to display that faith. In November 1836, Smith attempted to establish a bank, but political circumstances temporarily blocked him. In election after election, Smith had delivered the Mormon vote to the Democratic party; as a consequence, members of the rival Whig party in the Ohio legislature refused to grant his bank a charter. Undaunted,

In 1833, a mob destroys a Mormon printing office in Jackson County, Missouri. Thousands of Mormons, heeding Smith's teachings that Missouri was their spiritual homeland, had poured into the region, and friction soon arose between the Mormons and other settlers.

Smith simply named his institution the Kirtland Safety Society Anti-Banking Company and proceeded to operate the enterprise as if it were a bona fide bank.

By early January, questionable financial practices, combined with a nationwide economic crisis known as the panic of 1837, left Smith's outlaw bank teetering on the brink of failure. Smith and Young desperately struggled to save the institution, but by autumn it had failed. Many people, Mormon and Gentile alike, lost money. Leading Saints who were associated with the bank, including Smith and Young, were deluged by lawsuits from creditors.

The economic fiasco created dissension within the church. Prominent Mormons denounced Smith for spending too much time on matters of finance, in which he clearly was not competent. A movement grew within Kirtland, led by several members of the Twelve and other influential Mormons, to replace Smith as head of the church.

Young, ever loyal, was adamantly opposed to the scheme. At a meeting in the Kirtland temple, he denounced the dissidents. "I rose up," Young recounted, "and in a plain and forcible manner told them that Joseph was a Prophet, and I knew it, and that they might rail and slander him as much as they pleased, they could not destroy the appointment of the Prophet of God, they could only destroy their own authority . . . and sink themselves to hell."

Young's faction managed to maintain Smith's control over the church, but the situation remained tense and tenuous. The leaders of the anti-Smith group, including three members of the Twelve, were excommunicated (stripped of their church membership). The Kirtland temple, on which Young and many others had labored with such devotion, was auctioned off to help meet the financial judgments against the church. Worth about $40,000, it was sold for $150.

The Mormon world at Kirtland was collapsing around Smith and Young. On the morning of December 22, Young fled Kirtland, escaping his creditors as well as those who had lost money in Smith's banking scheme and were enraged by his unquestioning defense of the prophet. Leaving behind his wife, 5 children, and property valued at $4,000, Young arrived in Dublin, Indiana, where his brother Lorenzo and other Mormons were camped temporarily. Less than a month later, Smith, who left Kirtland for similar reasons, joined him.

Joseph Smith began the year 1838 in a state of despair and desperation. He had lost his temple, his printing press, many of his followers, and what little money he had. In a real sense, all he had left was Brigham Young. "Brother Brigham," he entreated his devoted supporter, "I am destitute and without means to pursue my journey. . . . I shall throw myself upon you and look to you for counsel in this case." Relief came when Young persuaded a prosperous local Mormon to donate $300 to Smith.

In February, Smith, Young, and a party of Saints left Indiana for the town of Far West, the center of Mormon activity in Missouri. About 8,000 to 10,000 Saints had settled between the Missouri and Grand rivers in the northwest corner of the state. Arriving in Far West in mid-March, Young bought some land, began farming, and sent for his family. In a short time, 1,000 Saints from Kirtland would join them.

As increasingly large numbers of Saints began to gather in northwest Missouri, the local Gentile population, fearing that the Mormons might dominate the area economically and politically, grew alarmed. Missouri frontiersmen, Young recalled, "rode from neighborhood to neighborhood making inflammatory speeches, stirring up one another against us." Some of the most militant Saints formed a secret paramilitary vigilante organization—the Sons of Dan, or Danites—to carry out revenge for attacks against Mormons. More moderate leaders such as Young feared that the formation of the Danites only would provoke further anti-Mormon violence.

By summer, a state of virtual civil war existed in Missouri between the Mormons and their Gentile neighbors. In

August, an armed scuffle ensued after non-Mormons tried to prevent Mormons from voting in a local election. No lives were lost this time. Mobs began burning Mormon haystacks and homes, and in late October three Mormons and one Missourian died in the Battle of Crooked River. Then, on October 30, 1838, an organized mob of more than 200 men stormed into a small, isolated Mormon settlement near Far

A woodcut depicts the massacre of Mormons at Haun's Mill on October 30, 1838. During a period of intense anti-Mormon violence in Missouri, heavily armed vigilantes raided the small Mormon settlement near the town of Far West. They killed 17 and wounded 15.

West and began shooting without warning or provocation. Seventeen Mormon men, women, and children were killed and 15 were seriously injured in this notorious attack, which became known as the Haun's Mill Massacre.

The governor of Missouri, Lilburn Boggs, an avowed anti-Mormon, soon called up the entire state militia. The Mormons, he declared, "must be exterminated or driven

In autumn 1838, Joseph Smith (in tent) agrees to stand trial for treason in return for the safe conduct of the Mormons out of Missouri. Smith appointed Brigham Young to organize the evacuation of more than 12,000 Mormons from the state.

from Missouri . . . for the public good." At that point, Joseph Smith realized that further resistance would end in a wholesale slaughter of his people. In exchange for the safety of the Far West settlement, Smith, his brother Hyrum and Mormon firebrand Sidney Rigdon surrendered to the authorities and agreed to stand trial for treason.

The arrest of the Smiths and Rigdon, along with the arrest, death, or defection of seven other members of the Quorum, meant that Young was the most important Mormon leader still free and connected with the church. From his prison cell, Smith appointed Young as president of the Quorum and made him responsible for organizing the evacuation of the Mormons from Missouri. Even if only temporarily, Brigham Young was now the de facto head of the Mormon church.

Through the fall and winter, Young oversaw the removal of between 12,000 and 15,000 Saints from Missouri to Illinois. As acting church leader, he became an obvious target for anti-Mormon vigilantes and was forced to leave

Missouri in mid-February 1839. He relocated his family to Quincy, Illinois, where he continued to supervise the exodus and resettlement and to direct the affairs of the church.

Meanwhile, at their trial, Joseph Smith, Hyrum Smith, and Sidney Rigdon had been found guilty of treason and ordered shot the next morning. The head of the militia, however, refused to carry out the execution, and the three languished in jail for nearly six months. They were finally able to escape by getting a guard drunk. Young and Smith were reunited in Quincy on May 3. It was, according to Young, "one of the most joyful scenes of my life." Young immediately relinquished his power and returned the reins back into the hands of the freed prophet and leader.

Young moved his family about 50 miles up, and across, the Mississippi River to Montrose, Iowa. On the other side of the Mississippi, at Commerce, Illinois—which Smith renamed Nauvoo, from the Hebrew word meaning "beautiful place"—the prophet had begun to build the largest Mormon city to date. The region, due to its marshy land and damp climate, was largely unsettled. In this unhealthy environment, many Mormons, including Young and his family, fell ill to cholera and ague, a malarialike sickness characterized by alternating chills and fever.

Nearly recovered by mid-September, Young, on Smith's orders, left his new home to lead the Twelve on an extended mission to England. Three years earlier, a Mormon mission had won about 1,300 English converts; by 1840 that figure had grown to nearly 1,700. Young traveled east, preaching throughout upstate New York and New England. He departed New York City for England on March 9, 1840.

Arriving in England in early April, Young discovered that the country was ripe for the teachings of Joseph Smith. England was in the midst of a deep economic depression. In a remarkable parallel to Brigham Young's own experiences 10 years earlier, many unemployed workers and impoverished farmers were seeking spiritual comfort. They found it in Mormonism. During his year in England, Young preached more than 400 sermons, visited the many scattered branches of the church, published the Book of Mormon and a Mormon hymn book, and established an official church periodical.

In the spring of 1841, Smith sent word for Young and the Twelve to return to Nauvoo, and they began their journey home in April. The mission had been a rousing success; in just one year, between 7,000 and 8,000 new converts had been baptized. In addition, Young initiated the migration of English Mormons to the United States, starting with 1,000 immigrants in June 1840. Over the next 6 years, more than 4,000 English Mormons would settle around Nauvoo.

For Young, the yearlong English mission represented a golden opportunity to prove not only his willingness to serve his church and his leader but also to demonstrate his skills as an administrator and organizer. Young arrived back in Nauvoo on July 1, 1841. But before he could be reunited with his family, which he had not seen since September 1839, Smith called a meeting with him and the other apostles. Smith told Young how much his hard work and sacrifice had impressed and pleased him. From this point on,

After fleeing Missouri, the Mormons established a new community, which Joseph Smith named Nauvoo, in Illinois. By 1844 the new Mormon sanctuary would have a population of about 12,000, making it the second largest city in the state at the time.

Brigham Young's status within the Mormon church was second in importance only to the prophet himself.

In 1841, Smith revealed to Young the most controversial doctrine of the Mormon religion, "celestial marriage" (or as it is more commonly known, polygamy), the idea that a man could—and *should*—have more than one wife at a time. According to Smith, Gentile marriage was a corruption of the holy state of matrimony, in which husbands abused and neglected their wife and children and engaged in illicit and immoral liaisons outside of marriage. Celestial marriage, he maintained, would resanctify the relationship between a husband and his wife (or, more accurately, wives).

The doctrine recognized two kinds of marriage—one that bound the husband and wife on earth and a higher form, performed in a temple, in which they were "sealed" for eternity. A woman could marry one man for life and yet be sealed to another for eternity. Men, however, could take an unlimited number of wives; indeed, Mormon polygamy stressed that a man's heavenly glory would be determined by the number of wives he took. Women also would be "saved" by celestial marriage. According to Smith's teachings, a woman could enter heaven only if she were married to someone endowed with the priesthood, that is, a loyal Mormon man.

Smith was convinced that celestial marriage was a biblical principle supported by the Old Testament and that Saints must practice it in order to restore the ancient ways as required by God. Smith had been secretly engaged in polygamy since 1835, and many of his detractors asserted that he developed the theological explanations merely to justify his own deviant sexual behavior. Polygamy would remain a controversial and divisive doctrine of the Mormon church until 1890, when church leaders officially discouraged Saints from observing the practice.

When Smith instructed Brigham Young to marry again, he was filled with morbid dread. "I was not desirous of shirking from duty . . . ," Young later admitted, "but it was the first time in my life that I had desired the grave, and I could hardly get over it for a long time." He realized the nature of the dilemma that he faced—either he must put aside his moral reservations and embrace polygamy or defy his leader and prophet and risk losing his position within Mormonism's elite and perhaps even his membership in the church. Eventually, he overcame his initial revulsion and accepted polygamy, reaffirming his commitment to Mormonism and Smith. In June 1842, the 41-year-old Young took his first plural wife, 20-year-old Lucy Ann Decker Seeley.

Historians and biographers differ as to the exact number of women to whom Young was married over the course of his life. Nevertheless, he is known to have had no less than 55 wives and possibly as many as 70. Many of these marriages were "in name only," but Young did father between 56 and 58 children by at least 16 of his wives.

Although the Mormon church officially denied the existence of polygamy until 1852, the church's elite, including Young, practiced plural marriage actively and frequently. Still, even after the doctrine finally was revealed, at its peak no more than 15 to 20 percent of all Mormon families were polygamous. Only about one-third of these polygamous families included more than two wives.

In January 1844, Joseph Smith decided to run as an independent candidate for the presidency of the United States. The campaign, he expected, would help publicize the religion and gain it additional converts. Young recruited more than 300 volunteers and dispatched them throughout the country to stump for Smith. He himself left Nauvoo on May 21 for an eastern campaign tour, arriving in Boston on June 16.

Smith's candidacy was launched during a period of serious internal conflict within the church. A group of dissidents who opposed polygamy and were excommunicated by Smith set up a rival Mormon organization in Nauvoo. The rebels published a newspaper, the *Nauvoo Expositor,* in

Lucy Ann Decker Seeley became Brigham Young's first plural wife in 1842. Young had grave reservations about Smith's doctrine of celestial marriage but was reluctant to defy the instructions of his leader and friend.

which they attempted to expose the prophet's alleged misdeeds. Outraged, Smith ordered the destruction of his opponents' press and all existing copies of the paper.

Smith's brazen violation of freedom of the press fueled anti-Mormon feelings in the Gentile communities around Nauvoo. Fearing the same kind of vigilante violence that had forced the Saints out of Missouri only six years earlier, Smith, his brother Hyrum, and two apostles gave themselves up to the authorities on June 25 to face charges of inciting a riot. They were held in the Carthage, Illinois, jail.

Campaigning in Massachusetts, Young later claimed that two days after Smith's arrest, of which he yet had no knowledge, he "felt a heavy depression of spirit, and so melancholy I could not converse with any degree of pleasure." It was not until July 16, 1844, almost three weeks later, that he finally learned the reason for this strange and

On June 27, 1844, a mob murders Joseph Smith at the Carthage, Illinois, jailhouse while the local militia—ordered to protect Smith—stands by idly. Smith's death profoundly affected the course of Brigham Young's life.

sudden rush of melancholia. On June 27, the day of Young's bout of depression, a well-organized mob had entered the Carthage jail, killing Joseph and Hyrum Smith and wounding apostle John Taylor. The other Mormon prisoner escaped injury.

The *New York Herald* predicted that Smith's murder "will seal the fate of Mormonism. They cannot get another Joe Smith." Indeed, the death of its charismatic founder sent

the church reeling. Who might be capable of succeeding him
as the spiritual and political guide of the Latter-day Saints?
Was there a man among them who would be able to help the
Mormon church overcome this devastating loss, heal its
internal divisions, and move it along its path toward the
Kingdom of God here on earth? Traveling night and day,
Brigham Young rushed back to Nauvoo, convinced that he
held the answer to these burning questions.

After Joseph Smith's assassination, Young convinced the Mormon congregation that the leadership of the church should be held collectively by the Twelve Apostles. Young quickly emerged as the church's real leader, and he was ordained church president in 1847.

5

Appointed by the Finger of God

IN THE 13 YEARS since he converted to mormonism, Brigham Young had proved himself a committed believer and skillful organizer. No man had been more loyal and devoted to the slain prophet, Joseph Smith. For five and a half years he had served as president of the Quorum of Twelve Apostles, the second most important position in the church. Young was certain that he should be the man to succeed Smith as the head of the Mormon church.

At the same time, another prominent Mormon, Sidney Rigdon, also wanted to fill Smith's shoes. Rigdon was a member of the church's ruling elite, the First Presidency, and had been a close personal friend of the prophet. In recent years, however, the two had drifted apart. Rigdon's opposition to polygamy had alienated him from Smith.

The matter came to a head at a special church conference convened on August 8, 1844, two days after Young's return to Nauvoo. Speaking first, Rigdon harangued the assembly for an hour and a half. He argued

Sidney Rigdon, an influential member of the church's ruling elite, sought to head the Mormon church after Joseph Smith's death. The congregation, however, chose Brigham Young and the Twelve Apostles to lead the church.

that he was the "ordained spokesman" for their martyred leader and insisted that he should serve as "guardian for the Church."

Then Young rose to address the gathering. He spoke calmly, claiming that the leadership of the church was not the right of one man but of the Twelve Apostles collectively. "I say unto you," he declared, "that the Quorum of the Twelve have the keys of the kingdom of God in all the world. The Twelve are appointed by the finger of God. . . . You cannot fill the office of a Prophet, Seer and Revelator: God must do this."

The congregation was moved deeply by Young's words. Many of those present even insisted that Young, as he spoke, began to assume the mannerisms, and even the physical traits, of Joseph Smith. It was as if their fallen leader had returned to place his mantle on Young's shoulders. When it came time to vote on who should lead the church, the conference selected Young and the Twelve nearly unanimously.

It soon became clear that Young had used this inspiring call for collective leadership to maneuver himself into the position of sole successor to Smith. As the president of the Twelve, Young was the most visible and influential, as well as the most forceful and capable, member of the body. He quickly emerged as the church's real leader. By the end of the year, he no longer was signing his letters, "Brigham Young, President of the Quorum of the Twelve," but "Brigham Young, President of the Church of Latter-day Saints."

For a time, Rigdon continued to challenge Young's authority, and Young also faced opposition from such men as James J. Strang, a brilliant and charismatic personality, and Joseph Smith's only surviving brother, William. Young, however, used his power to excommunicate these dissidents, which silenced them, at least within the boundaries of Nauvoo. Rigdon and Strang both tried to organize their own offshoots of Mormonism, and Strang was able to attract a sizable number of followers, perhaps as many as 10,000. Nevertheless, by end of the decade, neither one threatened Young's position.

In order to deal with this internal dissension, Young asserted what, in the eyes of his critics, was a dictatorial authority over Nauvoo. The Nauvoo police, consisting of between 200 and 300 loyal Saints, stifled all opposition. Whippings, known as "Aunt Peggy," were common. When faced with a challenger who questioned their authority, Young and Heber Kimball would warn, "He had better look out. I'll send Aunt Peggy after him."

So-called whittling societies were another effective means of discipline. A group of about 20 men would surround a troublemaker or suspicious outsider. Then, following their target wherever the person went, they would begin to slice shavings off wooden sticks with long bowie knives in such a way that the knife points ended up against the intruder's face. Intimidated, but not really harmed, the victim soon would flee, "whittled" out of town, as it were.

Having assumed Smith's position of power, Young connected himself to the prophet in another important way. Between September 1844 and May 1845, he took 15 more wives, 5 of whom had been married to Joseph Smith. The widows were to be Young's wives in this life only. According to the doctrine of celestial marriage, they were "sealed" to Smith in the next life.

By the end of 1844, the population of Nauvoo had swollen to more than 12,000, as hordes of Mormons from the East and England flocked there. Young announced that he hoped to promote in Nauvoo "every branch of industry and manufacture" and the "purchase of farms in the adjoining country." Conceiving of Nauvoo as a great Mormon city, he made the building of a sacred temple there a top priority. Young also realized that the temple, which was completed at the end of 1845, would serve to reinforce the continuity between Joseph Smith's leadership and his own.

Young's hopes for Nauvoo were dashed, however, when the Illinois legislature, responding to the rising tide of anti-Mormon sentiment in the state, revoked the city's charter in January 1845. The legislature's action fueled anti-Mormon violence, as mobs began burning Mormon houses. Young and the Twelve had no choice; they would have to abandon Nauvoo completely and build a new sanctuary somewhere on the vast frontier. Clearly, this daunting task was vital to the survival of the Mormon religion. Moreover, as Young well realized, the successful execution of this exodus would solidify permanently his position as the head of the Mormon church.

Young pondered several options. Texas, then an independent republic, was actively seeking American settlers. However, Mexico had claims on the region, and a military conflict appeared imminent. Young was reluctant to move his people out of the frying pan of religious persecution and into the fire of a war between Texas and Mexico.

He also considered the territories of California and Oregon, as well as Vancouver Island in the Pacific Northwest, as possible Mormon sanctuaries. Each was geographically remote and blessed with a mild climate, but each also had serious drawbacks. Oregon was inhabited by thousands of pioneers from Missouri; California was populated with a large number of both American and Mexican settlers. Young feared that a Mormon influx into either place would recreate the same conflicts that previously had forced them from Missouri and now was pushing them out of Illinois. In addition, the United States and England both had claims on Oregon and Vancouver Island. As in the case of Texas, Young did not want to be caught in the middle of an international dispute.

Nauvoo, Illinois, as it appeared in the 1870s. The town had flourished until bitter anti-Mormon sentiment and mob violence drove the Mormons from Illinois in 1846.

In 1867, a Mormon wagon train struggles through Utah's Echo Canyon. Young chose the Great Basin as the Mormon sanctuary because it was located more than 1,000 miles from the nearest white settlements, in the Missouri River valley and California.

Isolation, Young realized, was what the Mormons needed. Bitter experience had taught him that whatever place the Saints chose as their destination, they would have to be the first settlers—the first white settlers, that is.

As early as March 1845, Young began to consider the eastern rim of the Great Basin, specifically the valley of the Great Salt Lake in the region occupied today by the state of Utah. The Great Basin was a remote area about a thousand miles from the West Coast, uninhabited except for Native Americans. It belonged to Mexico, but because of its seclusion and arid climate it had been bypassed by both American and Mexican settlers and was not an area in dispute.

Young organized and oversaw every detail of the Mormon exodus, which, according to his instructions, was to

begin in the spring of 1846. Each family of 5, he proposed, should outfit itself with 1 strong covered wagon, 3 yokes of oxen, 1,000 pounds of flour, 1 bushel of beans, 2 pounds of tea, 5 pounds of coffee, and 1 keg of alcohol. (Two decades later, he would decree that Mormons should abstain from the use of alcohol and so-called hot drinks, meaning tea and coffee.)

Young recommended that in case of trouble, particularly from hostile Native Americans, every man should have a rifle or musket. However, he also advised each family to bring some goods to trade. A practical man, Young always believed that it was "better to feed the Indians than fight them." He told his people to take farming tools and 10 to 50 pounds of seed, so they would be ready to begin planting once they had completed their journey. By the end of November, 1,500 wagons had been built—with 1,900 more under construction.

In the midst of all this activity, Young was harassed by hostile state and federal officials. Charged with treason and counterfeiting, he managed to evade arrest throughout the fall and winter. Then, in January 1846, he received warnings that the federal government was planning to prevent the Saints from leaving Illinois. Faced with this threat to his plans, Young moved the departure date up to February.

On February 15, 1846, the Mormons began the first leg of their exodus west, their destination as yet undetermined (or at least undisclosed by their leader). Young knew that he had taken on a heavy responsibility. Still, leaving Nauvoo, he felt as if a massive weight had been lifted from his shoulders. In a letter to his brother Joseph, written on March 9, just 55 miles out of Nauvoo, Young declared, "Do not think . . . that I hate to leave my house and home. No, far from that," he assured his brother. "I am so free from bondage at this time that Nauvoo looks like a prison to me."

In mid-June, the Saints established Winter Quarters on the eastern edge of Nebraska Territory. Because their pace was quite slow and they were running low on provisions,

In 1867, the Joseph Henry Byington family rests during its migration to Utah. The Mormon family was following the trail blazed by Brigham Young.

Young decided that the best course would be to plant crops and wait out the winter in this place. By this time, Young had let his people know that he was leading them to the Great Basin; that was to be the site of the Mormons' new frontier home.

The winter of 1846–47 brought tragedy to the Mormon community. Epidemics of malaria and "black leg" scurvy took 600 lives, including 2 of Young's wives. Young, too, was in a constant state of ill health, the result, most of his associates believed, of overwork and fatigue.

Finally, on April 14, 1847, Young led the first company of 148 Mormons out of Winter Quarters. Traveling across 1,000 miles of barren plain and high mountains, the pioneers found their sanctuary on July 24 in the valley of the Great Salt Lake in the northwestern part of present-day Utah. Shortly after their arrival, Young, in his first letter from the Great Basin, happily announced "that every soul who left Winter Quarters with us is alive."

One week after they reached their destination, the pioneers, with geometric precision, began to lay out Great Salt Lake City (now known simply as Salt Lake City). The streets, 132 feet wide, formed square blocks of 10 acres. Each block was divided into eight lots, and each lot was to hold one house. Every other block would have four houses on its east and west sides but none facing north or south. The alternate blocks would have four houses on the north and south sides but none facing east or west. Houses on the same side of the street would be 132 feet apart, and every house was to be at least 20 feet from the street. The site of the proposed Mormon temple was located at the center of the town.

The towns of the Mormon frontier, of which Great Salt Lake City was the first, differed from typical frontier settlements in a number of ways. Most settlers were only 30 or 40 miles away from other outposts. Young, however, believed that the Mormons needed isolation. Other than Native Americans, their nearest neighbors, to the east and west, were 1,000 miles away. Moreover, most pioneers traveled west as individuals or in small units, whereas the Mormons migrated in large caravans. Finally, and most important, the Mormons, unlike most other western settlers, migrated for religious, not economic, reasons. They sought freedom to worship as they pleased. And so, instead of the competitiveness and rugged individualism that typified the "pioneer spirit," the Mormons exhibited an unusual degree of cooperation and concern for the general good.

In August 1847, Young and about 100 church members left the new city and headed back toward Winter Quarters to organize the next wave of migrants. Along the way, they met a company of 1,553 Mormons and thousands of assorted livestock already on their way west. The exodus was proceeding even faster than Young had planned or wanted; he had left instructions that only 400 should migrate that first season.

Returning to Winter Quarters at the end of October, Young decided to revive the church hierarchy created by Joseph Smith but left dormant since his death. Since August 1844, Young had been serving as the de facto president of the Mormon church. He now felt that it was time to formalize his position atop the church hierarchy.

The title page of William Clayton's Latter-day Saints' Emigrants' Guide. *The guidebook, published in 1848 to provide Mormons with information crucial to their journey to the Great Basin, provides one example of how well organized the Mormon migration was.*

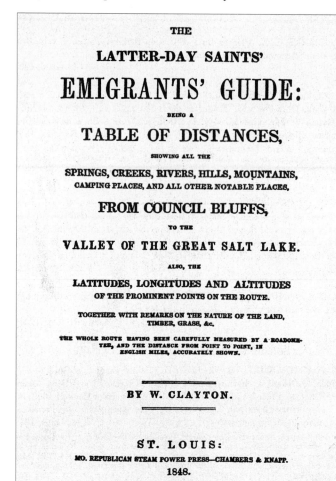

THE

LATTER-DAY SAINTS'

EMIGRANTS' GUIDE:

BEING A

TABLE OF DISTANCES,

SHOWING ALL THE

SPRINGS, CREEKS, RIVERS, HILLS, MOUNTAINS,
CAMPING PLACES, AND ALL OTHER NOTABLE PLACES,

FROM COUNCIL BLUFFS,

TO THE

VALLEY OF THE GREAT SALT LAKE.

ALSO, THE

LATITUDES, LONGITUDES AND ALTITUDES
OF THE PROMINENT POINTS ON THE ROUTE.

TOGETHER WITH REMARKS ON THE NATURE OF THE LAND,
TIMBER, GRASS, &c.

THE WHOLE ROUTE HAVING BEEN CAREFULLY MEASURED BY A ROADOME-
TER, AND THE DISTANCE FROM POINT TO POINT, IN
ENGLISH MILES, ACCURATELY SHOWN.

BY W. CLAYTON.

ST. LOUIS:

MO. REPUBLICAN STEAM POWER PRESS—CHAMBERS & KNAPP.

1848.

According to his proposal, he would be the church's prophet—the office held by Joseph Smith. Kimball and his own cousin Willard Richards would be his counselors. To-gether the three would make up the First Presidency. The following April, the church conference ratified Young's plan unanimously, and he formally assumed the title Prophet, Seer, and Revelator.

In May 1848, the new Mormon prophet left Winter Quarters with 1,229 Saints and again headed west. Several days later, Kimball departed with 662 more of the faithful. Young's company was nearly eight times larger than the pioneer party of the previous year and included many children and elderly people. Still, this second trek across the prairie took only 116 days—a mere 5 more than in 1847. Reaching the Salt Lake valley on September 20, Brigham Young never again would travel east of the Rocky Mountains.

Fortunately for the settlers of the initial company, the winter of 1847–48 had been relatively mild in the Salt Lake valley. However, when the snow did come, it piled high on the flat roofs of their houses, and once it melted, it leaked inside. In light of the hardships to come, this was but a minor inconvenience.

A series of late frosts the following May hit their crops hard; beans, cucumbers, melons, pumpkins, and squash all were damaged. But the worst was not over, for as summer neared, hordes of giant flying crickets ravaged the green corn and wheat fields, killing everything in their path. The pioneers tried flooding their fields in hopes that they might drown the insects, but there were just too many.

Then a flock of sea gulls from the Great Salt Lake suddenly swooped in and began to eat the crickets. The crickets had already done great damage, but at least some of the crops could be saved. The Mormons, convinced that the appearance of the gulls was nothing less than a miracle, commemorated the event with a bronze statue of a sea gull

This bronze statue in Salt Lake City honors the sea gull. When swarms of crickets began destroying Mormon crops in 1848, sea gulls from the Great Salt Lake devoured the insects. Enough of the harvest was saved to enable the early Mormon settlers to survive the harsh winter of 1848–49.

on the temple grounds. The statue still stands in Salt Lake City.

The frost, the plague of crickets, and the influx of new-comers created a severe food shortage. The extremely harsh winter of 1848–49 only made matters worse. Many Saints resorted to eating beef hides, wolves, dogs, skunks, and dead cattle in order to survive. To get his people through the winter, Young ordered strict rationing of all available foodstuffs. There was hunger, but no Mormon died of starvation. Years later, Young recounted the hardships of the early days in the Great Basin. "When I think of all that," he declared with much emotion, "I feel full of unspeakable tenderness for my people."

The year 1849 brought a renewal of the war between the crickets and the gulls; it also brought the California gold rush. When word that gold had been discovered in the Far West reached the Mormon sanctuary, Young feared that many of his people would join the stampede to the gold fields. A few Mormons did catch gold fever, but for the most part, Young's control over the faithful held them in place.

Salt Lake City, however, became a way station for the so-called forty-niners, the gold-mad prospectors who headed west in pursuit of riches. At first, the Mormons resented the intrusion. Eventually, as hundreds of these California-bound travelers began to stop at the Mormon town in search of supplies, wagon repairs, and fresh animals, the Saints realized they could drive a hard bargain with them. Young encouraged his followers to charge the best price possible for their goods and services. The California trade helped the Mormons establish an economic foundation in the Great Basin, ensuring their survival during these difficult early years.

Despite the hardships, the Mormon sanctuary grew rapidly. At the end of 1848, more than 5,000 Saints lived in the Great Basin; by 1850, the figure had doubled to more than

The Wasatch Mountains rise over Salt Lake City in this 1869 photograph. The Mormon community, following Young's instructions, quickly organized itself and began to expand rapidly. By 1850, 3 years after the first settlers arrived, more than 11,000 Mormons lived in the Great Basin.

11,000. Except for the forty-niners or perhaps a few trappers, traders, and Native Americans, they had few visitors. Parley Pratt, a leading Mormon official, described life in Salt Lake valley at that time. "How quiet, how still, how peaceful, how happy, how lonesome, how free from excitement we live," he declared.

When the Mormons first arrived in the valley, it still was Mexican territory. In February 1848, the treaty that ended the Mexican-American War ceded the region to the victorious United States. At that time, Young expressed his desire to President James K. Polk for a Great Basin territorial government. By early 1849, however, he hoped to bypass the territory stage and enter the union as a state.

With this in mind, Young established a provisional government and drew up a constitution for the proposed state of Deseret, named for the honeybee (a symbol of industriousness) in the Book of Mormon. Deseret, according to Young, was to encompass not only the area later known as Utah but a huge portion of the western states of today—northern Nevada and Arizona; much of Wyoming, Colorado, and New Mexico; southern California; and parts of Oregon and Idaho—in all, one-sixth of the total landmass of the continental United States. Naturally, Young was nominated to be the first governor of Deseret.

For the Saints, the road to statehood turned into a dead end. Excommunicated Mormons, such as William Smith, regaled the new president, Zachary Taylor, with stories about Mormon treason and polygamy (which at the time still was practiced in secret). Believing them, Taylor labeled the Mormons "a pack of outlaws . . . not fit for self-government" and promised to veto any bill for Mormon statehood that Congress passed.

But Taylor need not have worried. Congress ignored Young's ambitious statehood plans and instead proposed the creation of a much smaller territory named Utah after the local Ute Indians. (Federal officials felt Deseret sounded too much like the word *desert* and so had undesirable

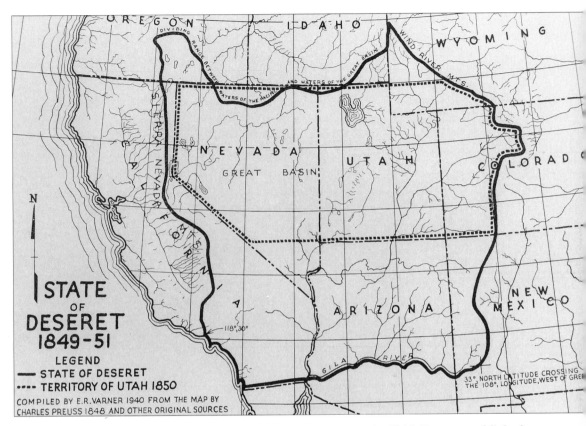

connotations.) The boundaries of Utah Territory encompassed the present states of Utah and Nevada and small portions of Colorado and Wyoming.

President Taylor died suddenly in July 1850. His successor, Millard Fillmore, was more sympathetic to the Mormons; on September 9, 1850, he signed the bill creating Utah Territory. The new law allowed the president to appoint the top territorial officials, and he filled these slots with a mixture of Mormons and Gentiles.

In selecting a territorial governor, Fillmore promised "not [to] appoint any man who was not friendly disposed towards" the Saints. Two months later, he delighted every loyal Mormon when he announced that the first governor of Utah Territory would be their own church president, Brigham Young.

In 1849, Young established the state of Deseret, hoping that it would be admitted to the Union. Congress ignored Young's scheme, creating instead the much smaller Utah Territory. President Millard Fillmore subsequently appointed Young governor of the territory.

The construction of the Mormon Tabernacle began in April 1863 as part of Brigham Young's plan to build God's kingdom in the Great Basin.

6

The Kingdom of God or Nothing

"IF BROTHER BRIGHAM TELLS ME TO DO A THING," vowed Heber Kimball, "it is the same as though the Lord told me to do it." Young's power over the Mormon faithful was absolute; critics charged that it was despotic. Utah Territory may have been "God's kingdom," but it also was Young's kingdom, and he ruled over it with unquestioned authority. There, a person's life belonged to the church and was controlled by the church's president, Brigham Young.

A key element of Young's power was the absolute control that he exerted over the church's missionary system. Although some Mormons volunteered for missionary work, most were selected for this duty by the president himself. At any time, Young might announce to the congregation that a certain churchman had been "nominated" for a two-year mission to the East Coast, England, South Africa, or even Russia. While the stunned nominee sat in silence, Young would ask all in favor to say aye, an empty ritual, because the congregation never opposed his wishes.

Of course, the hapless individual submitted to his call-ing—there was no real alternative. To defy the wishes of President Young would mean excommunication and expul-sion from the Mormon community, a devastating blow for a man who had staked his hopes for salvation on his mem-bership in the Mormon priesthood. There was also a practi-cal concern. If the man was a polygamist, Utah was the only place where he could live without running afoul of the law. So the reluctant missionary nominee obeyed his leader and departed for some faraway place, leaving his wives and children to fend for themselves.

Because missionaries were sent out, as the church put it, "without purse or scrip"—in other words, at their own expense—the Mormon church was able to increase its mem-bership at little or no cost. By the mid-1850s, the missionary system began to pay enormous dividends. In addition to its many congregations throughout England, the Mormons es-tablished branches in the Scandinavian countries, France, Germany, Italy, Switzerland, northern Africa, South Africa, India, the Far East, and the South Pacific.

The Mormon missionary system also provided Young with an effective means of handling potential threats to his authority. He simply invoked his absolute power of appoint-ment and sent political adversaries or personal enemies on one difficult mission after another. Back in Utah, whatever influence these opponents might have had among dis-gruntled or resentful Mormons was undermined. Young's position remained secure.

Shortly after the founding of Salt Lake City, Young began to organize the settlement of other parts of Utah (and ul-timately much of the West) in much the same way that he directed the church's missionary work. As with prospective missionaries, Young would call several families to move into an unoccupied region. He instructed them in every detail of settlement, such as building forts, cultivating crops, and dealing with the local Native Americans. After they reached their new site, the settlers would divert a stream or river in order to irrigate the field, build a combination meeting-house–schoolroom, and construct roads and dwellings.

When it created Utah Territory, Congress had cut drastically the boundaries of Young's proposed state of Deseret. Nevertheless, Young dispatched Mormon settlers to every corner of what he believed was the Saints' rightful domain. Mormon pioneers established a line of settlements from Salt Lake City in the heart of the Great Basin to San Diego on the Pacific Ocean. In all, the Mormons founded more than 325 western towns and cities. Even Las Vegas, Nevada, today a center of gambling and nightlife, originally was built by the sober followers of Brigham Young.

As Mormon settlements spread throughout Utah and the West, Young urged the church's European converts to

An 1876 oil painting by Frederick Dellenbaugh shows the fledgling Mormon settlement of Las Vegas. Under the direction of Young, the Mormons established more than 325 towns in the western United States.

At a dock in Liverpool, England, Mormons prepare to board a ship heading to the United States in the 1860s. In 1849, Young established the Perpetual Emigrating Fund, which enabled many impoverished Mormon converts in England and other European countries to immigrate to the United States.

gather in this booming sanctuary. Assembling the Saints in the United States became a church priority. When asked why Mormons could not live just as well in New York, London, Stockholm, or wherever, a Mormon official answered, "Because we should be in the midst of sin and wickedness and abomination, and it would be very difficult . . . to keep from being polluted by the evils which reign upon the earth at the present time." It was vital to the personal salvation of all Mormons that they live among each other, insulated from the corruption of the outside world.

Young realized that very few of his European followers could afford the trip from Liverpool, England, for instance, to Utah, which cost about 10 pounds. As the Mormon leader once noted, "very few indeed of those who have obeyed the Gospel have been possessors of wealth." To assist impoverished immigrants, Young established the Perpetual Emigrating Fund in 1849. Over the next two decades, the fund would finance passage to the United States for tens of thousands of European converts.

By 1852, with the Saints securely entrenched in their frontier enclave, Young decided that it was time to stop denying what had been rumored among the Gentiles for at least a decade—that the Mormons practiced polygamy. At a special Mormon conference in August he publicly acknowledged the practice. Because he was not a theologian, Young called on apostle Orson Pratt to deliver a spiritual defense of plural marriage. Ironically, less than a decade earlier, Pratt had resisted polygamy and was excommunicated for a brief time. He eventually recanted his opposition and was restored to full fellowship in the church, after which he loyally practiced polygamy.

Pratt defended the practice on a number of grounds, both lofty and worldly. He insisted that polygamy was necessary in order to populate the world with a large and increasing number of righteous people—in other words, Mormons. He also maintained that polygamy was practiced and divinely sanctioned in the Bible; Adam, Abraham, Isaac, Jacob, Moses, and even Jesus Christ, all, according to Pratt, took plural wives.

Further, Pratt argued that polygamy was justified because of "man's nature." Men, he asserted, had stronger sex drives than did women, and so polygamy provided a legitimate sexual outlet. Without it, men would resort to "whoredom, adultery, and fornication," as they supposedly did in the Gentile world. Women, on the other hand, because they had weaker sex drives, were naturally monogamous and needed no more than one husband.

The authority of the husband within the Mormon family was as unquestioned as the authority of Brigham Young within the Mormon church. "It is not the privilege of a woman," Young declared, "to dictate to the husband, and tell who or how many he shall take [as wives], or what he

In August 1852, Young called on apostle Orson Pratt to present a theological defense of the practice of plural marriage. Young had decided that Mormon polygamy should be publicly acknowledged.

shall do with them when he gets them, but it is the duty of the woman to submit cheerfully."

Finally, Pratt defended polygamy on legal grounds. The First Amendment of the U.S. Constitution, he noted, "gives the privilege to all inhabitants of this country . . . the free exercise of their religious notions." In other words, the highest law in the land supposedly protected the Mormons in their religious practices, including polygamy.

But despite Pratt's theological, biological, and legal justifications, the pragmatic Young perhaps had political reasons for promoting polygamy. In 1871, a writer for the *Salt Lake Daily Tribune*, a non-Mormon newspaper, offered valuable insight into Young's motives. "He, I believe, clings to polygamy," the reporter argued, "first, because he thinks it will more rapidly build up the Mormon state, and second, because its practice tends to isolate those who practice it from the outer world, keeps them together, and thereby renders his power more secure and stable." Indeed, to Young there was little difference between his spiritual leadership of the Mormon church and his political leadership of the Mormon people.

This cartoon, entitled "Waiting for the Old Man," shows Mormon wives chatting in their bedroom. Newspapers in the East often carried cartoons and stories that distorted the reality of the Mormon practice of plural marriage. These sensationalized accounts led to widespread condemnation of the Mormons.

Young's revelation of plural marriage prompted a moral outcry and provided ammunition for his personal and political enemies. Lurid, sensational, and grossly distorted stories about the sexual habits of the Mormons filled Gentile papers, amusing the curious, outraging the self-righteous, and titillating the repressed. Anti-Mormons, as well as many former Mormons, denounced Young for his supposedly lustful and lascivious character.

Many Gentile politicians compared polygamy in Utah Territory to slavery in the South. At its first national convention in 1856, the Republican party pledged to exterminate those "twin relics of barbarism—Polygamy and Slavery." On the other hand, the Democratic party, which had a stronghold in the proslavery South, defended the Mormons' "right" to practice polygamy. The Democrats maintained that each state or territory should be able to determine its own institutions.

Young, encouraged by the Democrats' apparently sympathetic position, endorsed their candidate, James Buchanan, in the 1856 presidential election. When Buchanan was elected in November, Young announced that he hoped the new president would be as friendly to the Saints as his two immediate predecessors, Millard Fillmore—who had originally appointed the Mormon leader governor of Utah Territory—and Franklin Pierce—who had reappointed him.

Through the early 1850s, hordes of Mormon migrants had continued to pour into Utah; by mid-decade, the number of Saints living in the Great Basin jumped sixfold, from 10,000 to 60,000. One-quarter of these came from England alone, with thousands more from Scandinavia, Germany, and Russia. To cut the costs of financing this mass migration, Young devised a scheme. Instead of the ox-drawn covered wagons that, until then, had brought the faithful to Utah, the church would supply two-wheeled handcarts. Three or four migrants would push each cart, which weighed between about 400 and 500 pounds when loaded, along the 1,300-mile trip from Iowa City, Iowa, to Salt Lake City.

Transporting their supplies and belongings by hand-cart, Mormon pioneers make their way across the Great Plains en route to Utah. Young devised the handcart scheme in the early 1850s to defray the cost of gathering the Saints in the Great Basin.

At first, Young's plan went smoothly enough. The first handcart company arrived safely in Salt Lake City by late September 1856. However, the next two companies ran into huge difficulties. Their handcarts were hastily constructed out of green lumber, which made the carts heavier and harder to push. Along the way, the lumber dried, causing the boards to shrink and the iron rims of the wheels to fall off. Because of these delays, provisions ran out. When the winter blizzards came earlier than expected, the travelers were stranded in the Rocky Mountains in Wyoming. In late November, a rescue party reached the unlucky migrants, but by then 200 of the 900 people had died of hunger or exposure.

Perhaps in his eagerness to gather the faithful, Young was not vigilant enough in overseeing the project. Perhaps he should have taken steps to assure that the carts were constructed better. Many people, both inside and outside the Mormon church, blamed him for the disaster. Young, never one to accept criticism readily, was defensive about the tragedy. "I do not believe," he answered his detractors, "the biggest fool in the community could entertain the thought that all this loss of life, time, and means was through the mismanagement of the First Presidency." In time, however, the scheme's successes outweighed this devastating failure. In all, more than 3,000 Saints managed to reach the Great Basin with their handcarts.

As governor of Utah, Young's relationship with the federal government always had been tense. From the first, he clashed with the Gentiles whom President Fillmore had appointed to positions in the territorial government. To the displeasure of non-Mormon federal judges, Young dominated and abused the legal system, interceding on behalf of Saints who had been charged with serious crimes.

Uncooperative and intimidating, the Mormons made life uncomfortable for Gentile judges and administrators. Some federal officials claimed that Young had revived the Danites, the secret paramilitary vigilante group, to harass them. In late 1851, three of Fillmore's appointees fled Utah, fearing for their lives; over the next six years, many other non-Mormon officials would depart Utah under similar circumstances.

By early 1857, Young's arrogance and a rising tide of anti-Mormon sentiment brought the Saints into direct conflict with the federal government. Senator Stephen A. Douglas, an Illinois Democrat who had been a friend of the Saints during their days in Nauvoo, denounced Young as a tyrant and reviled Mormonism as a "pestiferous cancer . . . gnawing into the very vitals of the [American] body politic." President Buchanan, facing intense criticism from Republicans in Congress and even from some members

In 1857, President James Buchanan decided to replace Young as the governor of Utah Territory. He secretly dispatched 2,500 troops to prevent any resistance to Young's removal. Young responded by mobilizing the Mormons to defend themselves.

of his own party—such as Douglas—for being too "pro-Mormon," decided to replace Young as governor of Utah Territory. To escort the new governor to his post and quell any potential resistance to the removal of Young, the president mobilized 2,500 troops and secretly dispatched them to the Great Basin.

In July, Young learned of Buchanan's action. His mind was filled with disturbing memories and anxious questions. He recalled the Mormons' expulsion from Missouri in 1838 and the evacuation of Illinois in 1846. Just 10 short years earlier, his people had founded their frontier sanctuary in Utah. Would they have to move again? Where would they go this time? Young soon realized that, given the pace at which the troops were moving, there was no time to organize a new migration. The Mormons would have to stand their ground against the power of the federal government; in the words of his favorite slogan, it was, "the Kingdom of God or nothing."

Meanwhile, as Young struggled to find a discreet and honorable way out of this approaching "Utah War," he suddenly was besieged on another front. During the fall of 1857, a party of migrants from Arkansas and Missouri traveled through Utah on their way to California. They made no secret of their dislike for Mormons; some even bragged about having participated in the Haun's Mill Massacre of 1838 and the 1844 lynching of Joseph Smith. To make matters worse, earlier in the year, apostle Parley Pratt had been murdered in Arkansas, the home state of many of these pioneers.

By the time the party reached the town of Cedar City, relations with the Mormons—as well as with the local Native Americans, whose livestock they had killed and wells they had poisoned—deteriorated to a dangerous level. Finally, a force of Mormon militiamen and Native Americans, organized and commanded by John D. Lee, a respected community leader, surrounded the migrants at a place called Mountain Meadows. Young had sent word to spare the

Gentiles, but his message arrived too late. Lee's vigilantes attacked, and virtually the entire party—between 100 and 120 people—was massacred. Only 18 young children were spared.

Although Young did not order this mass slaughter, he was, in a sense, responsible for it. A series of fiery speeches that he made just prior to the incident certainly encouraged the atrocity. For example, on the Sunday before the massacre, Young had denounced the Gentiles, declaring, "there is no just law requiring further forbearance on our part." Furthermore, although he knew who the responsible parties were, Young made no effort to punish them and actually protected them for many years. He counseled Lee: "Keep all secret as the grave. Never tell any one, and write me a long letter laying all the blame on the Indians." For many years this would be the Mormon church's official explanation for the Mountain Meadows Massacre.

In September 1857, with the U.S. Army breathing down his neck, Young issued a proclamation to his people: "Citizens of Utah—we are invaded by a hostile force." He declared martial law, called up the militia, and dispatched 100 "Mormon Raiders" to torment the army and, if possible, prevent its entry into the territory.

Young's guerrillas set grass fires, drove off the army's livestock, burned supply wagons, and torched two forts to prevent the troops from taking them. As the heavy November snowstorms came, the troops were bogged down and had to spend the winter in the mountains in Wyoming. These raiders continued to harass the army's supply trains, but by spring it was clear that the forces would survive and soon enter the Salt Lake valley.

Young hoped to avoid bloodshed but prepared for the worst. He ordered all Mormons living in northern Utah, including Salt Lake City, to abandon their homes and move south to the town of Provo. If necessary, Young promised, even more drastic action would follow. He would command the Mormons to evacuate the territory and destroy everything they left behind, just as the people of Russia had in 1812 as Napoleon's forces marched on Moscow.

Back East, as people learned of the sorry condition of the federal troops—thanks to Young's guerrilla campaign—previously supportive public opinion shifted against Buchanan. Influential newspapers and leading politicians in both parties began to call for an end to the ill-conceived conflict. Buchanan decided that he had to make peace with the Mormons and dispatched an envoy to meet with Young. For his part, the Mormon leader expressed his willingness to allow the new governor into Utah as long he came without the troops.

Negotiations began between the federal government and the Mormons. Buchanan's peace commissioners offered the Mormons a full pardon for their "seditions and treasons" if they accepted the new governor. The commissioners also asked the Saints to let the army in to "protect" the inhabitants. Young and his advisers were offended at being offered a pardon for a rebellion that, they maintained, was not their doing. Further, they rejected the absurd notion that the federal troops were there to protect the Mormons. The negotiations reached the point of collapse.

Young offered a compromise. He grudgingly accepted Buchanan's amnesty and agreed to allow the troops into the territory. However, they could not encamp in or near Salt Lake City. If these terms were violated, he warned, the Mormons would implement his scorched-earth policy. The new governor, Alfred Cumming, would be left with nothing to govern but a charred ruins empty of people.

On June 26, 1858, the troops marched through an empty Salt Lake City on their way to Camp Floyd, about 50 miles southwest. Once Young received confirmation that the army had come and gone, he allowed his people to return to their homes. In early July, Young proclaimed that the bloodless Utah War was over.

For the federal government, the whole affair had been a heavy-handed, mismanaged fiasco. For Young, on the other

hand, the guerrilla campaign, the evacuation of Salt Lake City, and the successful compromise added up to a major political victory. With just the right mix of resistance and diplomacy, he managed to prevent a bloodbath, demonstrate the solidarity of the Mormon people, and vindicate their religious beliefs.

Utah Territory may have had a new governor, but Young surrendered none of his real power. In fact, his steadfast leadership during the recent conflict only helped to increase his authority over the Mormon people. Governors would come and go, but until his death, Brigham Young, as president of the Mormon church, remained the de facto ruler of Utah, and his word still was law.

In the winter of 1858, federal troops on their way to Utah march through Wyoming during a snowstorm. Young eventually reached a compromise with the federal government, and the bloodless Utah War ended in July 1858.

A prodigious organizer and manager, Brigham Young involved himself in the minutest details of the vast Mormon community.

7

To Die in Harness

AS A NEW DECADE DAWNED IN 1860, the United States faced a deepening internal conflict, one that soon would erupt in civil war. In the 1860 presidential election, Buchanan's party, the Democratic party, was turned out of the White House. Young felt vindicated. After all, it was the Democratic candidate, Stephen Douglas, who in 1857 had suddenly turned against the Mormons and pressured Buchanan into the imprudent Utah War.

Nevertheless, Young did not welcome the Republican administration of new president Abraham Lincoln. The party was threatening to outlaw polygamy, and in Young's view, the new president "was no friend." In the 1840s, as Lincoln was rising through the ranks of Illinois politics, he, Young charged, "never raised his voice in our favor when we were being persecuted."

The divisive political issue of the day was, of course, slavery. In 1852, Young, motivated—as ever—by the desire to expand Mormonism, had managed to get slavery legalized in Utah Territory. He realized that the church would not win many converts from the South unless the Saints could assure slave owners that their "property"—that is, their slaves—would be protected in Utah.

Moreover, Young's personal views, like those of many whites at the time, were profoundly racist. In 1847, he had prohibited blacks from being ordained into the Mormon priesthood, a ban that remained in effect for 131 years. Young believed that blacks were inherently inferior to whites and suited only to serve, invoking Mormon doctrine to justify his racism. "The Negro is damned," he preached, "and is to serve his master till God chooses to remove the curse.... These are my views—and consequently, the views of all the saints—on abolitionism." Slavery, he told New York journalist Horace Greeley in 1859, is "of divine institution and not to be abolished."

However, once war broke out between the North and the South in 1861, Young affirmed his loyalty to the federal government. At the very time that the Southern states were seceding from the union, Young again applied for Utah statehood. "We [will] show our loyalty," he declared, "by trying to get in while others are trying to get out." At the same time, the Mormons also viewed the Civil War as the beginning of the end, the opening act of a great cataclysm in which war, famine, plague, earthquakes, and other natural disasters would culminate in the end of the United States and all earthly nations.

During the war, the federal government and the Saints attempted to cooperate. Asked about his policy toward the Mormons, Lincoln quipped, "Tell Brigham Young that if he will let me alone, I will let him alone." In the spring of 1862, the president requested that Young raise a militia to defend the Overland Stage—a key stagecoach route that ran between St. Joseph, Missouri, and San Francisco, California—against unfriendly Native Americans. The Mormon leader promptly obliged. Despite the apparent improved relations, the usual disputes between the Mormons and the Gentile territorial officials continued, and tensions, although held in check, remained constant.

Young founded the Mormon sanctuary in the Great Basin in the hope that through isolation and economic self-sufficiency his people would be able to build the Kingdom of God on earth. However, changes in American social and economic life during the 1860s began to erode the Saints' sweet dream of holy solitude.

First came the transcontinental telegraph line, a new communications link that brought the East and West closer together. Shrewdly, Young arranged a lucrative deal in 1860 to construct the final 1,000-mile stretch of the line,

In 1870, Utah Central Railroad workers pose outside the passenger station in Salt Lake City. Young organized the Utah Central Railroad to connect Salt Lake City with the transcontinental railroad and to provide jobs and economic growth for the Mormon community.

from Fort Laramie through Salt Lake City to California. The job was completed in 1861, and Young used the opportunity to establish his own Deseret Telegraph Company, which linked every major Mormon settlement to a central office—his own Salt Lake City residence.

Next, there was the transcontinental railroad. Young recognized that the enterprise presented an opportunity for profit and decided to take advantage of it. In 1868, he signed multimillion-dollar construction contracts with both the Union Pacific and Central Pacific railroads, creating jobs for destitute Mormons and enriching both his church's coffers and his personal fortune (which, in his 1859 interview with Greeley, he estimated to be around $250,000).

Young was disappointed when officials of the new railroad decided to bypass Salt Lake City in favor of a shorter route 50 miles to the north. However, he did convince them to make the Mormon city of Ogden the major terminal point for the line. In 1870, Young finished construction on his own Utah Central Railroad, connecting Salt Lake City with Ogden and the transcontinental line.

Young viewed the new railroad with hope and anxiety. It would, of course, make migration faster and easier and, thereby, assist his mission to gather the faithful. At the same time, however, he feared that it would bring an influx of non-Mormon ideas and goods into the Saints' sanctuary.

Hoping to safeguard the isolation that his people sought and cherished, Young instituted a series of schemes for Mormon economic self-sufficiency, designed to limit the flow of outside products. He also ordered a boycott of Gentile stores and products. "To trade with these miscreants," he instructed his followers, "is to trade with the devil; and he that trades with the devil is sure to sell his soul."

Not all of Young's construction projects were secular, however. In 1867, he oversaw the completion of the Mormon Tabernacle—a structure 250 feet long, 150 feet wide, and more than 60 feet high. Its interior, made entirely of white pine, holds 15,000 worshipers. The building still

serves as the spiritual center of the Mormon church and remains Salt Lake City's most famous and impressive landmark, as well as its most frequently visited tourist attraction.

By the mid 1860s, Young grew concerned about the thousands of dollars that left Utah Territory each year because Mormons bought tobacco and liquor products from the East that were of better quality than those produced locally. As early as 1833, Joseph Smith, in a divine revelation called the Word of Wisdom, had counseled his followers to abstain from the use of tobacco, alcohol, and hot drinks (coffee and tea). For decades, however, the Saints ignored Smith's revelation. Most Mormons, rugged, rough-and-tumble frontier people that they were, drank heavily and habitually smoked or chewed tobacco. Although Young enforced the Word in his own house, serving only milk and water at meals, he was known to enjoy a glass of beer on occasion. And, as the owner of two distilleries during the 1850s, he had profited from the production of liquor.

Young was never shy about invoking scriptural justifications to promote secular ends. In 1867, hoping to bolster his

Young supervised the construction of the Mormon Tabernacle, which was completed in 1867. The tabernacle still serves as the spiritual center of the Mormon church.

anti-Gentile boycott and stem the outflow of badly needed Mormon dollars from Utah, he revived Smith's Word of Wisdom and called for complete abstinence from tobacco, alcohol, coffee, and tea. To those who complained that they could not live without these things, Young replied, "Then die, and die in the faith, instead of living and breaking the requests of heaven." Still, he allowed local production of alcohol and tobacco for those who insisted on using it. Young's words may have been spiritual, but his motives clearly were economic.

The election of Republican Ulysses S. Grant to the presidency in 1868 signaled a return to old problems for Young and the Mormon church. Young had little regard for either the Republicans—who were longtime opponents of polygamy—or the new president. "Who goes to the White house in these days?" he asked with scorn. "A gambler and a drunkard."

Grant appointed a group of anti-Mormons to all the top offices in Utah Territory. For example, the new chief justice, James B. McKean, helped found the Republican party in the early 1850s and was one of the creators of its antislavery, antipolygamy platform. Likewise, on taking office, newly appointed Governor J. Wilson Shaffer announced his intention to subdue the Mormons and their powerful leader. "Never after me shall it be said that Brigham Young is Governor of Utah," Shaffer declared.

Through the summer and autumn of 1871, a federal grand jury charged a number of leading Mormons with violating a territorial statute that prohibited "lewd and lascivious cohabitation"—in a word, polygamy. In October, Young was arrested and indicted for having cohabited with 16 of his wives. He pleaded not guilty, posted a $5,000 bond, and was allowed to return to his polygamous home to await trial.

Young again had to appear in court in January 1872, this time to face a more serious charge—murder. William Hickman, a former Mormon and former bodyguard to Young, claimed that during the Utah War the Mormon president had

Opposite:

This composite photograph shows Brigham Young with some of his wives. In October 1871 a federal grand jury charged Young with violating a law prohibiting cohabitation. The charges were eventually dropped, but polygamy remained a controversial issue throughout Young's tenure as president of the Mormon church.

ordered him to murder a Gentile hunter and trader as revenge for hostile acts. This time, Young was denied bail and, because Salt Lake City had no federal jail, was confined to his home in the custody of a U.S. marshal.

Three months later, the Supreme Court ruled that the all-Gentile grand juries that had been used to indict Young and the other Mormons were drawn illegally. Both indictments—for lewd and lascivious cohabitation as well as for murder—were declared null and void. Young was set free along with the other accused Mormon polygamists. His legal problems were solved; no grand jury that included Mormons would indict Brigham Young.

William Hickman, Young's onetime bodyguard, claimed that the Mormon president had ordered him to murder a hostile outsider. The murder charges brought against Young based on Hickman's statements were dropped because no grand jury containing Mormon jurors would indict Young.

By the early 1870s, advancing years and chronic health problems began to take their toll on the once-vigorous Mormon president. In April 1873, Young, just 2 months short of his 72nd birthday, cut back his activities and went into partial retirement.

Young's retirement, however, was disrupted by a ghost from the past. For years the Mountain Meadows Massacre of 1857 had been shrouded in secrecy and rumor. Many people did not believe the official Mormon version of the story, which placed the blame for the massacre entirely on a band of Native Americans.

During his second trial for murder for his involvement in the Meadow Mountains Massacre of 1857, John D. Lee (seated, center) is surrounded by his lawyers. After being sentenced to death, Lee charged that Young was responsible for the massacre and covered up the facts afterward.

Finally, in 1875, John D. Lee, the vigilante ringleader, was indicted and tried—but freed when the trial ended in a hung jury. A second trial the following year, however, resulted in Lee's conviction, and he was sentenced to be executed. At this point, the Saints changed their story and, no longer blaming the Native Americans for the massacre, hung the whole matter on Lee. Young ordered Lee's excommunication from the Mormon church.

As he awaited death, the outraged Lee dictated his memoirs. In them, he accused Young of covering up the facts of the massacre, betraying him, and setting him up as the scapegoat. "Young has sacrificed me," Lee charged, "through his lust for power, after all I have done for him and the Mormon Church." Then, in a confession dictated to the *New York Herald*, Lee went even further, claiming that Young, because of his zealous and inflammatory teachings, was directly responsible for the massacre. There was at least some justification to Lee's charges. Naturally, Young, with characteristic vehemence, denied that he was an accessory either before or after the fact. Lee was executed on March 23, 1877.

As his 76th birthday approached in June 1877, Young declared that he was in excellent health and that "I calculate to die in harness." He spent the early summer traveling extensively, visiting Mormon towns north and south of the Salt Lake.

One August evening, however, Young's health took a sudden turn for the worse. He retired, ill, to his bed. His condition deteriorated steadily, and six days later he lay comatose. Late in the afternoon on August 29, 1877, the Mormon president opened his eyes, gazed upward, and called, repeatedly, the name of his prophet, mentor, and friend: "Joseph!" he exclaimed, "Joseph! Joseph!" Then, uttering a last gasp, Brigham Young died.

* * *

"But for Mormonism," Young told one of his daughters shortly before his death, "I would have [remained] a common carpenter in a country village." Still, as much as the Mormon church gave Young, he gave it much more in return. Without Young, Mormonism might never have survived the murder of its founder and prophet, Joseph Smith, much less endured as the potent religious force—with a worldwide membership of around 7.7 million—that it is today.

Neither a theologian nor a deep thinker, Young nevertheless possessed the right quality for the time and the task—the ability to lead and inspire large numbers of people. Few men, inside the Mormon church or outside it, had the talents to achieve what he did—to seize control of a besieged religion in a time of mortal crisis; to march thousands of believers to a place of safety; to bring thousands more from foreign nations into this sanctuary; to oversee the building of towns and cities, of telegraph lines and railroads; and to do battle with the most powerful politicians in the nation.

After his death, Young's successors realized that the federal government would not grant Utah statehood until the Mormons renounced polygamy. By September 1890, the church leadership decided that political recognition was more important than religious orthodoxy. Church president Wilford Woodruff issued a historic manifesto that declared, "We are not teaching polygamy or plural marriage, nor permitting any person to enter into its practice." The principle that Young would have defended with his very life and the life of his people had slipped from church doctrine into church history. Six years later, the new state of Utah entered the union. To this day, the Mormon church continues to exert a decisive influence, both spiritually and politically, over the state of Utah.

A profile published in the *New York Tribune* in 1865 offered rare insight, for the time, into the character of Brigham Young. Describing him as "a man of brains, quick

The announcement for Brigham Young's funeral describes the particulars of the procession. Young died on August 29, 1877, at the age of 76.

ORDER OF PROCESSION

AT THE

Funeral of President Brigham Young,

New Tabernacle, Salt Lake City,
SEPTEMBER 2d, 1877.

Tenth Ward Band.

Glee Club.

Tabernacle Choir.

Salt Lake City Council.

President Young's Employes.

President Joseph Young, Bishop Phineas H. Young, Bishop Lorenzo D. Young and Elder Edward Young.
(President Brigham Young's brothers.)

THE BODY,
Borne by Clerks and Workmen of Deceased.

Ten of the Twelve Apostles as Pall Bearers.

Counselors of President Brigham Young.

The Family and Relatives.

First Seven Presidents of the Seventies.

Presidency and High Council of Salt Lake Stake of Zion

Visiting Presidents, their Counselors and High Councils of Various Stakes of Zion.

Bishops and their Counselors.

High Priests.

Elders.

Lesser Priesthood.

Seventies.

The General Public.

——:o:——

Brigham Young relaxes in 1875, two years preceding his death. Under Young's skillful leadership the Mormons built an impressive, thriving community that stretched throughout the Great Basin.

intuitions, good judgment and untiring industry," the article observed that "he would doubtless have achieved great success in politics, trade, manufacturing, or almost any other walk of life."

Indeed, Young was an important religious leader, but he also was much more—a colonizer, a statesman, an entrepreneur. To his detractors, he also was a tyrant, a charlatan, and a scoundrel. As the head of the Mormon church during the most turbulent period not only in its history but in the history of the United States as well, the dynamic and controversial Brigham Young was—and had to be—all of these things.

Further Reading

Arrington, Leonard J. *Brigham Young: America's Moses.* New York: Knopf, 1985.

Bringhurst, Newell G. *Brigham Young and the Expanding American Frontier.* Boston: Little, Brown, 1986.

Carmer, Carl. *The Farm Boy and the Angel.* Garden City, NY: Doubleday, 1970.

Gottlieb, Robert, and Peter Wiley. *America's Saints: The Rise of Mormon Power.* San Diego: Harcourt Brace Jovanovich, 1986.

Hirshson, Stanley P. *The Lion of the Lord: A Biography of Brigham Young.* New York: Knopf, 1969.

Morgan, Dale L. *The Great Salt Lake.* Lincoln: University of Nebraska Press, 1986.

Robertson, Frank C., and Beth Kay Harris. *Boom Towns of the Great Basin.* Denver: Sage Books, 1962.

Taylor, P. A. M. *Expectations Westward: The Mormons and the Emigration of Their British Converts in the Nineteenth Century.* Edinburgh, Scotland: Oliver & Boyd, 1965.

Chronology

1801	Born in Whitingham, Vermont, on June 1
1804	Family moves to the western frontier of New York State
1815	Mother, Abigail Young, dies of consumption
1817	Brigham Young leaves home; apprentices as a carpenter, painter, and glazier
1824	Marries Miriam Works
1830	First sees the Book of Mormon
1832	Baptized into the Mormon church; wife, Miriam Young, dies; Brigham Young travels to Kirtland, Ohio, to meet Mormon leader Joseph Smith; leaves on a mission to Canada
1833	Makes a second mission to Canada; moves his family from Upstate New York to the Mormon settlement in Kirtland, Ohio
1834	Marries Mary Ann Angell
1835	Appointed by Smith to the Quorum of the Twelve Apostles
1837	Forced to leave Kirtland after Mormon bank failure
1838	Arrives in Far West, Missouri; appointed president of the Twelve by Smith; organizes the Mormon evacuation of Missouri
1839	Moves his family to Iowa
1840	Departs the United States for a mission in England
1841	Returns from his successful English mission; settles in the Mormon center of Nauvoo, Illinois
1842	Marries his first plural wife, Lucy Ann Decker Seeley
1844	Becomes the de facto leader of the Mormons after the death of Joseph Smith
1845	Completes the construction of the Nauvoo temple; decides that the Mormons must establish their own sanctuary on the western frontier

1846   Organizes the Mormon exodus out of Nauvoo

1847   Leads a pioneer company of 148 Mormons from Winter Quarters to the Great Basin; arrives in the Salt Lake Valley on July 24

1848   Officially ratified as the Prophet, Seer, and Revelator of the Mormon church; leads a second party of 1,229 Mormons from Nebraska to Salt Lake City

1850   Appointed the first governor of the newly created Utah Territory by President Millard Fillmore

1852   Reveals the Mormon practice of polygamy

1856   Organizes the tragic handcart migration from Iowa City, Iowa, to Salt Lake City, during which 200 European Mormon immigrants die

1857   Replaced as territorial governor by President James Buchanan; participates in the cover-up of the Mountain Meadows Massacre; declares martial law in Utah as federal troops try to enter the territory

1858   Orders the abandonment of northern Utah; resolves the conflict with the federal government and welcomes the new governor into Utah

1867   Revives Smith's revelation, the Word of Wisdom, instructing Mormons to abstain from alcohol, tobacco, coffee, and tea; oversees the completion of the Mormon Tabernacle in Salt Lake City

1868   Secures contracts for work on the transcontinental railroad

1871   Indicted for violating antipolygamy law

1872   Indicted on murder charges and held, under guard, in his Salt Lake City home; both indictments dropped after the Supreme Court rules that the grand juries were impaneled illegally

1877   Dies in his Salt Lake City home on August 29

Index

American Fur Company, 20
American Revolution, 26
Angell, Mary Ann. *See*
    Young, Mary Ann
Auburn, New York, 30

Bear River valley, 12
Black Hills, 20
Boggs, Lilburn, 55
Book of Mormon, 37, 39, 49,
    78
Bridger, Jim, 21–22
Buchanan, James, 87, 89–90,
    92, 95

Calvin, John, 40
Camp Floyd, 92
Carthage, Illinois, 11, 61, 62
Central Pacific Railroad, 98
Church of Jesus Christ of
    Latter-day Saints, 11, 39.
    See also Mormon church
Civil War, 96
Commerce, Illinois, 57. *See
    also* Nauvoo, Illinois
Crooked River, Battle of, 54

Deseret, 78
Deseret Telegraph Company,
    98
Douglas, Stephen A., 89, 90,
    95

Erie Canal, 31

Far West, Missouri, 53, 54–55
Fillmore, Millard, 79, 87, 89
Fort Bridger, 20, 22
Fort Laramie, 20, 98

Genoa, New York, 28, 30
Goodyear, Miles, 22
Grand River, 53

Grant, Ulysses S., 100
Great Basin, 12, 15, 22, 23, 70,
    72, 75, 76, 77, 78, 83, 87,
    89, 90, 97
Great Salt Lake City. *See* Salt
    Lake City
Greeley, Horace, 96, 98
Greene, John P., 42

Harris, Moses "Black," 21, 22
Hastings Cutoff, 22
Haun's Mill Massacre, 90
Hickman, William, 100, 102
Hopkinton, Massachusetts,
    25, 26, 27

Independence, Missouri, 46
Iowa City, Iowa, 87

Jackson County, Missouri, 49

Kimball, Heber Chase, 15, 41,
    42, 43, 46, 50, 67, 75, 81
Kirtland, Ohio, 43, 45, 46, 47,
    49, 50, 51, 52, 53
Kirtland Safety Society Anti-
    Banking Company, 52

Laman, 38, 39
Lamanites, 39
Lee, John D., 90, 91, 104
Lehi, 38, 39
Lemuel, 39
Lincoln, Abraham, 95, 96

Mendon, New York, 32, 42,
    43, 44
Methodist Episcopal Reform
    Church, 34
Mexican-American War, 13,
    78
Mississippi River, 23, 57
Missouri River, 12, 53

Mormon, 39
Mormon church, 11
    doctrine, 40–41, 59
    expelled from Missouri,
        11, 49–50
    founded, 39–40
    missions, 81–82
    renounces polygamy,
        105
    settles in Great Basin, 12,
        23
    world congregations, 82
Mormon Tabernacle, 98–99
Moroni, 38, 39
Mountain Meadows Mas-
    sacre, 90–91, 103

Native Americans, 15, 39, 70,
    71, 73, 78, 82, 90, 96, 103
Nauvoo, Illinois, 11, 12, 18,
    23, 57, 58, 60, 63, 65, 68,
    71, 89
Nauvoo Expositor, 60
Nebraska Territory, 71
Nephi, 38
New York Herald, 62, 104
New York Tribune, 105–6

Ogden, Utah, 22, 98
Omaha, Nebraska, 12
Ontario, Lake, 32
Oregon Trail, 20, 22
Oswego, New York, 32
Overland Stage, 96

Palmyra, New York, 37, 49
Pawnee Indians, 18, 19
Perpetual Emigrating Fund, 85
Pierce, Franklin, 87
Platte River, 20
Polk, James K., 13, 78
Port Byron, New York, 31, 32

Pratt, Orson, 85–86
Pratt, Parley, 78, 90
Provo, Utah, 91

Quincy, Illinois, 57
Quorum of Twelve Apostles,
    50, 51, 56, 57, 65, 66

Rigdon, Sydney, 56, 57, 65–
    66
Rocky Mountains, 12, 15, 75,
    88

Salt Lake City, Utah, 73, 77,
    82, 83, 87, 88, 91, 92, 93,
    98, 99, 102
Salt Lake Daily Tribune, 86
Second Great Awakening, 32–
    33
Seeley, Lucy Ann Decker. *See*
    Young, Lucy Ann
Sioux Indians, 18, 19
Smith, Hyrum, 11, 56, 57, 61,
    62
Smith, Joseph, 12, 41, 47, 49,
    58, 65, 66, 67, 68, 74, 75,
    90, 104, 105
    arrest and trial in Illinois,
        61
    arrest and trial in Mis-
        souri, 56, 57
    birth, 37
    establishes Mormon
        church, 39–40
    murder of, 11, 62–63
    physical appearance, 43
    religious experiences and
        visitations of, 38, 99

reveals doctrine of
    "celestial marriage"
    (polygamy), 59
runs for president, 60, 61
and settlement in
    Kirtland, 43, 45, 46,
    50, 51, 52, 53
similarities to Brigham
    Young, 37–38
Smyrna, New York, 27, 28
Strang, James J., 67
Supreme Court, U.S., 102
Sweetwater River, 20

Taylor, Zachary, 78

Union Pacific Railroad, 98
Utah Central Railroad, 98
Utah Territory, 79, 87, 90, 95,
    99, 100
Utah War, 90–92, 95, 100, 102
Ute Indians, 21, 78

Washington, George, 26
Whitingham, Vermont, 25, 27
Winter Quarters, 12, 14, 18,
    19, 71, 72, 73, 74, 75
Woodruff, Wilford, 105
Word of Wisdom, 99–100
Works, Miriam. *See* Young,
    Miriam

Young, Abigail "Nabby"
    (mother), 25, 26, 27, 28,
    29–30
Young, Brigham
    arrested, 100, 102
    becomes head of Mor-
        mon church, 11, 56

birth, 25
death, 104
as governor of Utah Ter-
    ritory, 79, 89–90
joins Mormon church, 42
marries, 31, 47, 60
meets Joseph Smith, 43
organizes move from
    Nauvoo to Great
    Basin, 12, 70–71
and polygamy, 59–60
retires from presidency,
    103
and slavery, 95–96
Young, Clara (wife), 15
Young, Clarissa (sister-in-
    law), 41
Young, Elizabeth (daughter),
    32, 46
Young, Fanny (sister), 37, 42
Young, John (brother), 33, 42
Young, John (father), 25, 26,
    27, 28, 29–30, 37, 42
Young, Joseph (brother), 33,
    42, 43, 44, 71
Young, Lorenzo (brother), 15,
    42
Young, Lucy Ann (wife), 60
Young, Mary Ann (wife), 47
Young, Miriam (wife), 31, 32,
    41, 42, 43
Young, Nancy (sister), 42
Young, Phinehas (brother),
    33, 37, 41, 42
Young, Rhoda (sister), 42
Young, Vilate (daughter), 32,
    46

Zion's Camp, 50

PICTURE CREDITS

Bob Bernotas is a freelance writer. He holds a Ph.D. in political theory from The Johns Hopkins University and has taught philosophy and political science at Morgan State and Towson State Universities. He has written four previous books for Chelsea House, *The Federal Government: How It Works*, *The Department of Housing and Urban Development*, *Amiri Baraka*, and *Sitting Bull*, and numerous articles on jazz and sports. He lives in New York City.

Vito Perrone is Director of Teacher Education and Chair of Teaching, Curriculum, and Learning Environments at Harvard University. He has previous experience as a public school teacher, a university professor of history, education, and peace studies (University of North Dakota), and as dean of the New School and the Center for Teaching and Learning (both at the University of North Dakota). Dr. Perrone has written extensively about such issues as educational equity, humanities curriculum, progressive education, and evaluation. His most recent books are: *A Letter to Teachers: Reflections on Schooling and the Art of Teaching*; *Enlarging Student Assessment in Schools*; *Working Papers: Reflections on Teachers, Schools, and Communities*; *Visions of Peace*; and *Johanna Knudsen Miller: A Pioneer Teacher.*